FROM THE FLIGHT DECK

the diary of an airline pilot

Nigel Knot

NERTHUS

First published in Great Britain in 2023 by Nerthus

A CIP catalogue record for this title is available from the British Library.

ISBN 978-0-9955034-3-4

Printed and bound by Amazon

Published by Nerthus

For Pen
Thank you for putting up with me

WHY I WANT TO BE A PILOT
By Anon, aged ten

When I grow up I want to be a pilot because it's a fun job and easy to do.

That's why there are so many pilots flying around these days.

Pilots don't need much school.

They just have to learn to read numbers so they can read their instruments.

I guess they should be able to read a roadmap too.

Pilots should be brave so they won't get scared if it's foggy and they can't see, or if a wing or motor falls off.

Pilots have to have good eyes to see through the clouds, and they can't be afraid of thunder or lightning because they are much closer to them than we are.

The salary pilots make is another thing I like.

They make more money than they know what to do with. This is because most people think flying a plane is dangerous, except pilots don't because they know how easy it is.

I hope I don't get air-sick because I got car-sick, and if I get air-sick I couldn't be a pilot and then I would have to go to work.

(First published in the South Carolina Aviation News)

1987

I was sitting in an armoured personnel carrier, covertly hidden in the middle of a wood in northern Germany during the Cold War. A pilot in the RAF, I had been seconded to a nonflying tour working with the British Army's Sixth Armoured Brigade as an air liaison officer, and this tank without a gun was my office away from my office.

We had been on exercise for a week and I was feeling a little grubby. I was also being slowly pickled by the various noxious fumes emanating from the fried food-engorged soldier manning the comms station. We had agreed - well, as it was the military, I guess it had technically been an order, but I didn't work that way - that if he needed to break wind he should go outside. It seemed this latest miasma was seeping through his pores and I was stuck with it, and it was stuck to me.

The lack of fresh air was making me feel sluggish, so when the brigadier's driver arrived, slightly out of breath, I couldn't understand what he was trying to say to me. I could see his eyes had started to water, so I suggested we speak outside. I was leaving the military and had applied for a job with a large British airline. Apparently, a letter had arrived at my German home, inviting me for an interview in three days' time, and, as it was to be their last interview process for the foreseeable future, it was a question of now or never. My wife, Penny, knowing how important this was, had somehow managed to track me down, and had asked the driver to bring me home. During the drive back, it dawned on me that either Pen had the sleuthing skills of Sherlock Holmes or we were rubbish at hiding in woods.

But I am getting ahead of myself. My journey towards a career with the airlines began many years before that. Aged five, I was obsessed with the TV show The Thunderbirds. I was adamant I was going to pilot 'Thunderbird One' at some point in the very near future. All I needed to do was walk like a puppet and perfect moving my eyes quickly from left to right. How hard could that be?

As I entered my teenage years, my yearning to fly was as strong as ever. But my parents did not have £100,000 lying around for me to attend a private flying school, and my Saturday job wasn't coming close to covering it either. There was only one thing for it: I would try and join the RAF and hope that they would teach me how to fly for free.

Fast forward ten years, and I found myself the captain of an RAF Chinook helicopter on a tour in the Falkland Islands, testing out the theory that penguins will fall over backwards as they watch you fly overhead (it's a myth; they don't).

My years in the RAF were a mixed bag. I loved the flying, it was exhilarating, like nothing I'd known before or since.

And I made some life-long friends. But I was a square peg in a round hole, a rebel at heart, resistant to authority in general, and to taking orders in particular. And I hated battling against the RAF's petty rules and regulations – being dragged in front of the Wing Commander and formally bollocked for getting married and buying a house without his permission was a particular low point.

I reasoned a career with an airline would allow me to fly without being constantly at odds with my employer. So over the first two years of my ground tour with the Army, I had been quietly and methodically wading through the process of obtaining my commercial pilots' licences, taking leave to return to the UK for the seemingly never ending stream of exams and flight tests. (Not a single one involved me walking like a puppet.)

There was no going back. I'd given notice to resign my commission twelve months ago, as required by aforementioned regulations, and would soon be unemployed. I urgently needed a regular pay-check to feed our growing family, and cope with our terrifyingly high mortgage repayments (interest rates were a staggering fifteen percent in the late 1980s.)

Anyway, to return to the British Army's armoured personnel carrier hidden in a wood in Northern Germany. Against all the odds, I managed to catch my flight to London for the first in a series of interviews with the airline. By the time I made it to the third interview stage I was a civilian, now living in the UK. The recruitment panel might have sensed my desperation. I'd spent my first month's unemployment benefit on a new suit in the hope of making a good impression. Or perhaps the gods were smiling on me, because the airline offered me a job – as First Officer on the Lockheed L-1011 TriStar.

1990-1995
TriStar First Officer

The **Lockheed L-1011 TriStar** was a medium-to-long-range, wide-body trijet airliner. Unusually, our company used it on both the long-haul and short-haul networks. Crews could fly to Greece 'there and back' on one trip, and enjoy a three day stop-over on a Caribbean island the next. The TriStar was the third wide-body airliner to enter commercial operations, after the Boeing 747 and the DC-10. It had a seating capacity of up to 400 passengers and, depending on the variant, a range of 4,000 to 6,000 miles. Its three engine trijet configuration had one engine under each wing, along with a third embedded in the tail and the upper fuselage.

For its time, the TriStar featured a highly advanced autopilot system and was the first wide-body to receive certification for a completely blind landing capability in zero-visibility weather. It was an accepted convention in our airline, when reporting the performance of this automated landing system in the flight log, just to write PFM. Everyone, including the engineers, knew this was short for Pure Fuc#ing Magic. And it was.

Crunch Time

I'd flown helicopters for most of my RAF career, so the thought of flying a proper big aeroplane made me feel both nervous and excited, as if I'd finally grown up. But first, I had to pass my flying training course. Today's modern flight simulators are good. So good in fact that it's possible to do all your training and testing in them, right up to the point where you are ready to fly the real thing with fare paying passengers. That's right - the guy up at the pointy end could be on his very first flight.

Thirty years ago, however, the technology wasn't quite so realistic. After the simulator training, we were required to take a real aircraft, with real empty seats, to a real airport. Our aim was to try and demonstrate our competence as aviators either until we cost the airline too much money and we were axed, or until we proved we were safe to be let loose on the paying public.

Eight of us trainees set off with three training captains to Shannon Airport, Ireland; the airport of choice for 'base training'. It had all the facilities, was relatively quiet, and in jet terms, wasn't too far away. I was delighted to be chosen as the co-pilot for the short flight from Heathrow to Shannon. It meant that on our arrival there, I was already in the pilot's seat and would be the first to fly the circuits.

A circuit is basically a take-off, a race-track pattern back to the runway, and a landing. It's a precisely defined manoeuvre, and tests all the basic piloting skills in a short space of time: take-off, climb, level off, acceleration, turning, timing, power handling, speed control, weather and wind awareness, checklists, gear and flap handling*, deceleration, descent, approach and landing - all in a ten-minute frenzy of activity.

But instead of a normal landing, to save time we were doing 'touch and goes'. As soon as we touched down, the flight engineer would reconfigure the flaps, set take-off power, and we would hurtle down the runway for another take-off before you could draw a breath. It meant that if you didn't keep up, even for just a few seconds, the aircraft would start doing things you weren't ready for, and things would go very wrong very quickly.

The TriStar was designed with enough power to cope with its normal payload of 400 people, cargo and fuel for an international flight. But that day, in Shannon, devoid of almost all those things, it was very lively. One of the things I discovered that day was that events happen very quickly in a big jet aircraft.

One of the things the other seven trainees discovered was that in an empty aircraft at take-off power, the acceleration and climb gradient was so pronounced that if you happened to be sitting on a plastic tray near the flight-deck at the start of the take-off, you could toboggan all the way down to the back. And as it was a twin aisled aircraft, you could have a race.

After an exhausting fifty minutes, and five take-offs and landings, I was 'done' in every sense of the word. But, mercifully, I had passed and was released for commercial flight.

*Without getting into too much detail, because even basic aircraft aerodynamics is a book in itself, flaps are used to increase the lift generated by the wings, allowing for safe, slower flight and shorter take-off and landing distances. Because they also cause drag, they are retracted when not needed. Likewise, because of the massive amount of airborne drag they produce, the gear or undercarriage is tucked away in the belly of the aircraft when not needed.

It's My First Time

My very first flight out of training came out of the blue. I mean, who could possibly have predicted there would be an uncovered seven-day trip over the Christmas period? I can only imagine the trainee first officer originally rostered for it must have been very sick indeed to pass up on that one. Anyway, they needed a replacement first officer and I needed a first sector. Off to Africa - Accra via Kano, it was then.

As the father of two small children, you can imagine how wretched I felt about being away over the entire Christmas period. So Pen and I decided there was only one thing for it. If Easter was a moveable feast, then why shouldn't Christmas be the same? It took some frantic, last-minute organising: hurriedly written letters to Father Christmas asking him to come two days early. Phone calls to bemused parents and in-laws asking them to throw some stuff into a suitcase, and hit the motorway now.

We celebrated Christmas Day on December 23rd, and we made it work. And Father Christmas made it work – and I am eternally grateful to him. As it turned out, I would be away for many more official Christmas Days over my thirty-year career, but I never once felt as if I'd missed out on the magic. (Apparently, Jesus was actually born in January anyway.)

I drove away from a house full of over-excited children, a frazzled wife and exhausted grandparents, and arrived at Heathrow to an equally packed flight deck: the training captain, flight engineer, a safety pilot, and me.

In those days, all long-haul aircraft carried two pilots and a flight engineer. Flight engineers sat just behind the first officer's position on the right-hand side of the flight deck and managed the fuel, hydraulic, electrical and pneumatic systems. They excelled at hands-on tasks such as refuelling and the myriad of practical issues that arose during a flight, including unblocking the soon-to-be-obsolete chemical toilets.

They also farted a lot, ate all the chicken crew meals and had an encyclopaedic knowledge of where to go for a post flight beer and a cheap breakfast the following morning, anywhere in the world.

They have since been replaced by hidden black boxes of electronic trickery, which means most of the aforementioned systems are now managed automatically, and require only occasional intervention from the pilots. It also means the flight deck has lost some great characters, but it is now so much less smelly. And, of course, there is a fighting chance of getting the chicken curry.

Safety pilots were required for the first few flights to support the busy training captain, and provide an overview. Things must have gone reasonably well because I can't really remember much of the day, except for the landing into Kano. I was flying the TriStar for the first time with passengers and, clearly, my experience of landing a very large passenger aircraft was limited. Well, as you know, it was *very* limited. I'd flown the simulator and I'd completed five circuits in an empty aircraft at Shannon - in broad daylight, onto a runway that had all the latest radio navigational guidance systems to help with the correct approach path. It also had approach lighting, touchdown lighting, runway edge lighting and centreline lighting *.

In sharp contrast, darkness had fallen, and Kano only had runway edge lighting; information I hadn't spotted on the airfield charts beforehand. It's also 1,500 feet above sea level, and hot. Well, it's Africa, so I guess you'd expect it to be hot. But at 'hot and high' airports, the air density is much less than at an airport in a temperate climate at sea level. Say Shannon, for example. And low-density air makes the instruments mis-read **. The aircraft is always higher, and more crucially, faster than the readings on the instruments.

The combination of these two instrument errors meant a higher-than-normal rate of descent was required, and things were happening even faster than normal. I was about to land a plane in the pitch black of an African evening and all I could see was the outline of a long box made out of lights, which represented the runway. Well, it *was* the runway.

Without any other visual reference, as the aircraft changed its position in space, the box floated around the windshield. And it was approaching very quickly. The training captain was sitting in the other seat, unlit pipe in his mouth, as if he was at home in his slippers. I was in the other seat, quite frankly working really hard, my overloaded brain desperately trying to make sense of a meagre amount of visual information. This was not some PlayStation game where I could simply have another go. I had to get this right.

There are no prizes for guessing that my very first landing with passengers was more like a controlled crash without the controlled bit. At a height of 30 feet the pilot's aim is to reduce the rate of descent to produce a smooth touchdown. I failed to do this, and we hit hard.

Even the training captain was sufficiently stirred to utter, 'I say'.

As we were taxiing onto the stand, Sally, the crew member who had looked after us during the flight, came onto the flight deck.

'That was a firm landing,' she said casually.

I glanced back at her, my eyes cowed in embarrassment, only to notice her nylon stockings were concertinaed around her ankles. Jest delivered, she turned to leave, but not before adding, 'by the way, you made most of the oxygen masks drop down'.

Looking back at that day, it makes me realise just how far we have come as a bunch of professional aviators. Now we are taught to 'project, trap and mitigate'. To project ahead, and cover the enormous number of possible permutations and combinations presented to us. To verbalise all these issues, come up with solutions and create a plan, long before such an 'event' could ever happen.

So, thinking back to that evening, if Popeye sitting next to me had said, whilst sucking on his pipe, 'by the way old boy, don't forget the effects of low density. Oh, and there's a hump on the runway, try not to hit it', I am fairly confident things would have gone a lot more smoothly.

*All these lights are designed to give the pilot perspective on vertical and lateral positioning with respect to the correct approach path and touchdown point on the runway.

** Barometric instruments are three of the four most important flight instruments a pilot uses to build a picture of what the aircraft is doing. They use outside air pressure and density to relay information to the pilot. The three instruments are: the altimeter to show altitude above the reference point; indicated air speed, and vertical speed indicator which displays the rate of climb or descent. They are calibrated using an internationally agreed standard value of sea level temperature and pressure. Any deviation from that standard figure will result in errors in their readings. We know all about those errors and can adjust our actions accordingly - unless we are on our first flight and so maxed-out we forget.

Metal bars, Malaria and Parasitic Worms

There was a delay in Kano as the resident ground engineer re-stowed the oxygen masks and carried out a heavy landing check, so named for self-explanatory reasons. With nothing damaged apart from my confidence and self-esteem, we continued our journey to Accra. After complaints from some of the passengers, and as it was in no-one's interests to give everyone a repeat pummelling from me, the captain flew the sector and did the landing.

Clearly, being able to land an aircraft correctly comes quite high in the top ten essential skills of a pilot. And we had a whole week before our return flight - a painfully long time for me to dwell on my failings.

After landing at Accra, the captain taxied the aircraft to the stand in his usual calm (and dare I say, detached) manner. As he turned the plane into the parking area, I noticed a large metal scaffold bar, hanging vertically from a chain on the centreline of the stand. I figured it had fallen from the gantry, and the captain was heading straight for it. Concerned, I glanced at him but there was no response. I turned around to look at the engineer, raised my eyebrows and flicked my head at the metal bar but again, no response. We were getting closer and closer to it, and at this rate we were going to stove in the nose of the aircraft. Eventually I could sit there no longer.

'STOP!' I shouted.

The captain reacted immediately, stamped on the brakes and the aircraft came to a shuddering, violent stop.

'What's the matter? What is it?' he asked.

By now I was totally confused. I pointed at the bar.

'There, look there, haven't you seen it? That metal bar, you're about to run into it!'

'Yes of course I can see it,' the captain replied. 'We are supposed to nudge it with the nose of the aircraft. It tells us we are in the right place to park. I know it's a bit basic but it seems to work. Should I proceed now do you think?' he added with a kind smile.

I thought I'd had it all back at Kano, but it seemed humiliation had not finished with me just yet.

It was my first visit to Africa and I was spellbound. Dusty cars on unmade roads; heavily-ladened, bare-footed people drifting everywhere and nowhere, at a pace that suggested nothing was that important. Roadside vendors seemingly in no rush to sell their few wares, and nobody in a great rush to buy them either. The heat, the flies, the feral dogs and cats. Men sitting in the shade smiling and chatting; ladies in their colourful dresses carrying babies in papooses, and expertly balancing inconceivably large loads on their heads. It all sounds a bit of a cliche but there it was, unfolding in front of me.

I spent the first couple of days acclimatising to this new way of life by sitting by the pool, and swimming.

'You shouldn't be swimming,' one of the crew informed me.

'Why not?'

'Bilharzia.'

I had read the company's health warnings on this particular region of Africa. I knew that Bilharzia was an infection contracted when fresh water parasitic worms burrow into your skin and lay eggs. But this was a posh hotel with chlorinated water and I hadn't seen too many of the other guests writhing around in agony at the poolside, so I reasoned it was relatively safe.

The crew were taking no chances though. I resolved to let a few days go by and then mention that if they really did think the water unsafe, then showering in infected water carried just as much risk. I would then sit back and watch as they either scratched their skin off with hypochondriac imaginings, or they became the great unwashed.

A more immediate and present danger, of course, was malaria. Malaria avoidance in those days involved medication before, during and after a trip. It was the norm for stomachs to rebel against the pills and, coupled with heat, humidity, different food, time changes and nights out of bed, it made for an uncomfortable and often messy existence.

Certain fleets were regular visitors to malaria hotspots, meaning some crews never really had a break from the medication or its effects.

Taxi!

On one of our rest days in Accra, the flight engineer said he was going to a local market and invited me to go along. He said it was just a short taxi ride away, so I accepted. As a total newbie and invited guest, I was keen to fit in, so when he said we needed to walk a short distance to get a taxi, I didn't ask why we couldn't just order one at the hotel. Ten minutes later and a little damp under the collar, we came to a small square with a tired-looking car parked half in the shade.

'This is it,' he said.

I got into the back, while he went to speak to a chap sitting on a chair not far away. It was very hot in the car. After a moment, the engineer joined me. We waited. And we waited.

'Where's the driver?' I asked, shaking sweat out of my eyes.

'He's over there, sitting in the shade.'

I gave the engineer a confused look.

Just then, another man climbed into the front passenger seat. He didn't acknowledge us. He just sat there.

'What's going on and why are we not going anywhere?' I asked.

'Well,' said the engineer, 'there's a two-tier fare structure. Top tier, we have the taxi exclusively. I've gone for the second tier.'

'Which is?'

'We sit here until the taxi is full.'

'But that will mean waiting for enough people who all want to go in the same direction as us.'

'Exactly,' said the engineer with a pitying look that questioned why I was struggling with the concept of the West African taxi tier system.

'But that could take ages!' I was starting to panic about being trapped in this oven forever. 'How much are we saving doing it this way?'

'Well, we're sharing the total cost, so for the two of us, it's half price.'

'OK, but how much are we saving?'

'About a pound.'

So, for a saving of one pound, we couldn't set off because we were still waiting for a fourth passenger who, for all I knew, was just finishing his lunch or his thesis on why flight engineers were such tight arses.

'I'm going to wait outside then.'

'No, you can't do that,' said the engineer, slight panic in his voice. 'The only way of reserving your place is by being physically in the car.'

'How about we cut our losses, upgrade to the higher tier, and offer the gentleman in the front seat a free ride?' I pleaded.

'That would almost certainly cause offence.'

'Yes, to your back pocket,' I muttered to myself. 'I'll pay.'

'No -'

'OK. Well thanks for the invite and it's been a lovely experience but I'm going back to the hotel now.'

'You can't go because that will mean I have to wait for another passenger to take your place.'

I peeled my back and legs off the plastic car seat, and gave him a look that said I really did understand the concept of his taxi tier system and, to be honest, I just didn't care.

Two Stripes and You're Out

New first officers only have two stripes on their epaulettes. I hated this as it made me feel insignificant. I felt it broadcast to the world that I was a newbie and inexperienced, and I guess it would be hard to argue with that considering my recent performance in Africa. Pilots must have four years' experience in the airline before becoming a senior first officer and achieving that third stripe.

It was my second trip and we had just arrived at the hotel in Manchester. The foyer was busy, and I noticed that our presence had sparked a certain amount of interest from the general public. Many pairs of eyes were taking in the imposing figure of the captain, striding confidently towards reception with his four stripes and hat adorned with 'scrambled-egg' silver braid. Next up were the cabin crew who were all young and female. They were getting quite a few looks too.

But I appeared to be totally invisible.

Likewise, the flight engineer. To be honest, flight engineers were never worth looking at. They always exhibited a dishevelled 'I'm not interested in all this bollocks' aura, which seemed to go perfectly with their crumpled uniform jackets and mangled uniform hats which were never, ever, worn but stuffed into the top of their flight bags.

I knew that crew were often given fast-track check-in, so I loitered to see what the procedure was here. I quickly caught a man's eye and was delighted at the show of recognition on his face. Perhaps I wasn't so invisible after all. He walked up to me and handed me a key. I was surprised, but relieved I wouldn't have to join the long check-in queue.

'Would you take my bags to room 223 please, porter,' he said, and walked away.

New York, New York

Civilian flying was proving to be a totally different world to military life. In the RAF, we lived in tents if we were away on exercise. And if we were on base, we spent our days in a basic office block adjacent to the hanger. The hanger had its own distinctive smell of petrichor, aviation fuel and bitter-sweet hydraulic fluid. The Chinook helicopter had its own gritty aroma too. It was basically a utility vehicle to ferry equipment and soldiers about – men and women who had been in the field for a week or more, without access to a shower block.

Flying rations were a cardboard box containing a sandwich, a packet of crisps and a hard-boiled egg. And, for some inexplicable reason, there was always a small pack of garibaldi biscuits (the ones that look as if they are mixed with dead flies).

By contrast, with the airline there would be a beautifully laid out cheese board waiting for us on the flight deck at the start of every trip, followed by a succession of beautifully presented crew meals that didn't involve a single garibaldi biscuit. And we stayed in real hotels with real beds down-route, not under smelly canvas.

I was very excited about my next trip. My first time flying to New York was also going to be my first time across the Atlantic. A typical route across the Atlantic involves a sea crossing between Ireland and Newfoundland, some 1700 miles, taking you beyond the range of conventional radio, air traffic control and navigational beacons. To compensate for the lack of ground-based active controlling, a system of airways (or tracks) is drawn up on a daily basis to take advantage of the predicted winds for that particular day.

There are usually six to eight such tracks running parallel and separated from each other by one degree of latitude, which is 60 nautical miles. Aircraft crossing the Atlantic are assigned one of these tracks and have to join it at a pre-agreed height, speed and time. And they are required to make certain points along that track, called waypoints, at a specific time to ensure there is adequate separation between aircraft ahead and behind on the same track, and at the same level. This means hundreds of aircraft can safely cross the Atlantic each day.

I was still in training but my performance so far meant I no longer needed a safety pilot. We were now operating as a 'natural' crew of two pilots and a flight engineer. This was another career milestone: flying a long-haul aircraft across the Atlantic to the United States of America. And it was thrilling to be handed over to a controller who spoke with a real American accent.

America is a country so vast that if you live there, there is never anything else over the horizon but more America. The distance from New York to San Francisco is about 2500 miles, which is the same distance as London to the North Pole and not far off London to Kuwait. It is a country that is uncompromisingly confident with itself. Do you remember Ye Olden Days, when scholars thought the earth was the centre of the universe and everything else revolved around it? Well, that's America.

Their national sport is a combination of rugby with impressive padding, and Sumo wrestling. It's a game only played in America and yet it's called the World Series. It should come as no surprise then that they have their own unique way of organising commercial aviation. But more of that later.

On the flight over, the flight engineer mentioned he and the captain were hiring a car to go sightseeing in New York State and he invited me along. I was torn because I had never been to Manhattan and was looking forward to seeing the sights. He assured me that we went to New York so often I would soon be sick to death of the place, but this was a one-off opportunity to venture outside the city. I was persuaded and accepted his offer.

Crew on stop-overs around the world were given an allowance, in the local currency. In the 1990s it was a simple procedure of walking up to the hotel receptionist, who would furtively glance left and right, reach under the counter, and slide a plain brown envelope towards you with a knowing nod. All very cloak and dagger stuff. To all intents and purposes, it was invisible cash, not linked to UK earnings or tax. In countries with rampant inflation the envelope would be quite sizeable, resembling those exchanged by drug cartels in TV dramas. In reality there was probably enough in there to buy a couple of breakfast sausages and a beef burger for lunch.

I mention this because it turned out our fine upstanding gentleman of a flight engineer was on a mission. His wife didn't know it yet, but she was soon to become ex-Mrs Flight Engineer. He was doing lots of American trips, buying any spare dollars off the crew, and stashing it all away in a secret bank account he had opened in the US, away from the prying eyes of any future divorce lawyers. And the reason for the car trip was not sightseeing but property searching. He was planning on buying a place in America, which he also hoped to keep beyond the reach of the lawyers. The day out consisted of me sitting in the backseat of the hire car like a twelve-year-old child listening to the two adults in the front seats bitching about their wives. We didn't see any of the promised glorious New York State scenery but just a series of small depressing hovels, potential boltholes from the flight engineer's divorce proceedings. It was probably one of the most disheartening days of my working life. And I didn't even get a bag of crisps to keep me amused while the adults were busy. At least they left the car window slightly open for me.

And Manhattan remained unexplored. To rub salt into the wound, just after this trip, New York as a destination was taken from the TriStar and given to the Boeing 747. I didn't get the chance to be sick to death of it. It would be fifteen years before I visited New York again.

And on Today's Menu...

I was still fairly new to the TriStar, but I felt I was now on top of the 'day job' of flying the beast. We had been chartered by the MOD to take a large consignment of cargo from Luton to Cyprus. Having positioned the empty aircraft to Luton, we were now waiting for the load to be delivered. At one o'clock, we were sitting around with not much to do when the crusty old flight engineer announced he was hungry. As it was a cargo flight, we had no cabin crew. He said he wasn't going to play cook, and told me to put the meals in the oven. Technically, as first officer, I was second-in-command of the aircraft, and he shouldn't have told me to do anything. But being a new two-striper, this was clearly not going to wash. I explained I'd never operated the ovens before and he replied sympathetically, 'You're a bright lad, figure it out'.

Very kind of him, I thought.

The TriStar had been designed with many new ideas and features, including placing the galley in the belly of the aircraft to maximise passenger seating. To get down there, there were two lifts, and I was rather pleased with myself when I managed to operate them. Now down in the underfloor galley, I started the process on groping around for a light switch, finding the master power switch, selecting an oven from the huge bank of possibilities, finding its power switch, and scrabbling through the trollies for our food. It all took a long time because I had never been down in the galley before and had no idea what I was doing. But it gave me perverse pleasure to think of the engineer growing hungrier and hungrier as time went on.

I found the trays of food, placed them in the oven and set the timer. I then went back up to the flight deck where I received the inevitable sarcastic comment that I could have made the meals from scratch in the time it had taken to put them in the oven.

Fifteen minutes later the smoke alarms sounded on the flight deck indicating a possible fire in the galley.

'Lunch is ready then,' said the engineer

Grabbing his torch and fire extinguisher, he set off at speed towards the lifts. Five minutes later and all made safe, I was invited back down to the galley to inspect my work.

The inside of the oven was reminiscent of a work by Salvador Dali, familiar shapes melted and distorted into grotesque new forms.

'You are only supposed to put the foil food containers in the oven, not the plastic trays as well, you half-wit.'

I had assumed they were heat resistant Bakelite trays. The oven was clearly beyond repair, but the thing that really annoyed the engineer was not a fire that could have written off a £100M aircraft, but the fact his lunch was ruined.

Well, That's First Class

I had been called out on standby to position* to Orlando via Miami with a captain and flight engineer. We were to fly a TriStar back from Orlando to London after engineering work to fix a technical issue. The second positioning sector from Miami up to Orlando was with a domestic American airline. Our industrial agreements state that whenever we position, we are booked business class or better. So, the three of us were sitting in an MD 80 in what they called first class. In fact, it was a single row of slightly larger seats, but I wasn't complaining.

After completing her pre-flight safety drills, a cabin crew member sat down in the folding 'jump-seat' opposite us for take-off. It could have been a classic British awkward moment, but she seemed unfazed by the fact the three of us were looking directly at her. With typical American 'openness' she quickly discovered we were flight crew and off she went with airline banter.

The sector was short, on a par with Gatwick to Manchester. During those flights, our cabin crew would serve drinks and a hot meal in a frenzy of activity. So, I was a little confused when, after take-off, she didn't immediately spring from her seat to start the in-flight service.

'You're not keen to start the service then,' I joked.

'Honey, I'm here to save ass, not kiss it,' she replied.

Fair enough.

Eventually, she stood up and asked if we wanted a drink.

'We'll all have a glass of champagne please,' said the flight engineer, not bothering to ask us.

'I'll just have a beer thanks,' I corrected him.

Drinks dispensed, she then started the meal service. This consisted of her moving down the cabin at a constant speed whilst repeating the words, 'nuts or pretzels, nuts or pretzels,' flinging them left and right like one of those clay pigeon throwers.

Ten minutes later she was back, dragging a black bin liner behind her and collecting the empty plastic cups and wrappers. Halfway down the cabin I noticed she had caught the bottom of the bin liner on something sharp. It had a hole in it, and was depositing rubbish back into the aisle almost as quickly as she was collecting it. This didn't seem to bother her or slow her progress. She left the trail of debris where it fell, like an over exuberant Hansel in Grimm's fairy tale.

Finally, exhausted by all this activity, she returned to her seat.

'What exactly is the point of first class?' I asked, observing we had received nothing more or less than the rest of the aircraft.

'Honey,' she said, 'you got a proper glass.'

*Sometimes crews are required to fly one way as a passenger. Americans often refer to this as deadheading. Our company called it positioning.

Hide and Seek

When I first joined the company thirty years ago, there was a definite hierarchy in car ownership. And not as you might imagine. The young and single first officers, who had plenty of disposable income, drove around in brand-new Porsches. The older first officers and newer captains who by this time had mortgages and families to support were lucky to be driving around in a five-year-old Audi or BMW. But you could always spot the senior captains because they had clapped-out Ford Escorts or Penny Farthings. They were not only supporting a mortgage and family, but also several other mortgages and families from their third or sometimes fourth marriages. Back then, it seemed to be a disease that targeted these middle-aged men.

I'd just arrived at the crew car park and was talking to Pete, who typified that group. He was rapidly approaching fifty. Assuming the grass could be greener, he had binned his marriage and set up shop with a late-twenties female crew member.

Whilst we were chatting, a young first officer parked up in an uncharacteristically modest Honda. He thought it necessary to tell us it was his 'airport car', something to be left in the crew car park without having to worry about his proper car being damaged. Pete looked at his own scratched and dented wreck and said, 'This is my airport car too. Depressingly it's also my only car. Things aren't likely to change either. Julie wants a baby. Thing is, I've already got lots of children. I've done all that parenting business, thought I'd finished with it all.'

'Yes', I said, 'but Julie's only twenty-nine. You can't blame her for wanting children of her own.'

'I suppose so. Who would've thought it?'

'Yeah, who would've thought it?'

I fitted into a different category, having already had a previous career. I arrived with a young family, lots of mortgage and little disposable income. So instead of a flash car, I drove a tired-out Ford Mondeo. Which was fine, because neither Penny nor I were particularly interested in cars. As long as they worked, they were good enough. Only thing was, they didn't really work. Pen drove an ancient, three-door Renault 5. To gain access to the rear seats' occupants, she had to force open the driver's seat locking lever. Once a child had been extracted, she would then bludgeon the lever back into position using a hammer I had thoughtfully provided for this very purpose.

On one occasion, she had just dropped the kids off at school and was using percussive persuasion on the driver's seat when one of the more precious mothers walked by. She stopped and said, 'Oh Penny, it's you, I thought you were one of the nannies or something. Where's your real car?'

At the time Pen was beating the crap out of her car, I was busily driving my very tired Ford Mondeo into the ground. The air-conditioning wasn't working, nor was the CD player, the rear electric windows or indeed any of the so-called driver conveniences. The tires were just about legal, the windscreen wiper rubbers were in shreds but the biggest issue was that the catalytic converter had just failed. This meant that the engine couldn't breathe properly and the exhaust back-pressure built up to such a degree that the car wouldn't go over thirty miles an hour. I resolved to squeeze one last trip to Gatwick out of it before consigning it to the scrapyard.

After I landed back from said trip, which was another overnighter, I'd been up for the better part of twenty-four hours. Fatigue was making the world start to swim and as I reached the car park I began to panic. I couldn't remember where I'd left the car. The weather was hideous; bitterly cold, high winds and heavy rain. Having just come back from the Caribbean, I didn't have a coat. I trudged down every row, getting thoroughly soaked in the process, and failed miserably to find my car. Had someone stolen it? But why, when the only thing less enticing was the half-full skip in the corner. I paddled back to the entrance, walked into the security staff building and, with water dripping off my nose said, 'I can't find my car. It might have been stolen'.

With a lilting Welsh accent, the security guard replied, 'I hear that almost every day. Had a tiring night, have you?'

He reached for his waterproof jacket and handed me a large golfing umbrella. 'Come on, I'll help you look for it. Leave your bags here,' he added with a kindly smile.

As I was already soaked, the umbrella was going to be pretty useless but it was such a kind gesture I nearly hugged him. Of course, we found my car fairly quickly. I don't know why I couldn't remember where I'd left it, because it was under the only tree in the car park; a tree that was clearly a firm favourite with the local bird population. By the look of things, they had had a wonderful time shitting on my car for the last three days. I've no idea what birds eat in the Gatwick area, but their droppings looked pretty robust stuff.

Setting off for home, I was cold and wet and the heater wasn't working so I kept my uniform jacket on in a futile attempt to warm up. The wipers were doing a splendid job of smearing the rain around the windscreen and with every pass, they bumped over the hardened pieces of bird shit. It made a wonderful replacement beat for the non-existent CD player. Because of an accident on the M23, I was forced to go through Reigate. If you're familiar with Reigate, you'll know the road out of the town up to the M25 is long, windy and steep. I had only just started up the hill when it became obvious the car wasn't coping. Fifth gear, fourth gear, third gear and foot flat to the floor, the engine working hard against the collapsed catalytic converter, I was managing a pretty decent twenty-three miles per hour. Cars were streaming past me in the overtaking lane, clearly irritated by my snail's pace.

A few hundred yards later, as I craned forward, peering through the bird crap, a large tree bow, brought down by the high winds, smashed onto the bonnet of my car. One of its branches lodged under a windscreen wiper and held fast.

Another car using the overtaking lane slowed down, probably intending to give me grief for going so slowly. As I turned to look at them, I realised the passenger was stared at me in wide-eyed disbelief. I was not projecting the best ambassadorial image for the company. I was still wearing my wet uniform jacket. I was shivering, eyes bloodshot and deeply bagged, with stubble on my chin, and driving at twenty-three miles an hour in a clapped-out car, garnished with bird shit and the major part of a tree.

I couldn't even manage to feel embarrassed; I was too tired. I turned back to peer through the front windscreen, slump shouldered and dejected. I gave the slightest of Gaelic shrugs, said to myself, 'ehh', and carried on stoically up the hill, shedding leaves as I went.

Nowadays of course, phones have GPS which memorise our cars' locations. But back then the multi-storey carpark at Heathrow offered an even greater challenge than the carpark at Gatwick: a much greater choice of spaces in which to lose the car. And being multi-storey, the choices were in 3D.

It was after another of those jet-lagged wanderings, as I was putting my bags in the boot, that I noticed one of the crew using the bonnet of someone else's car to rest her large suitcase on.

She saw me looking and said, 'saves me having to lift it twice'.

That was OK then.

Another time, a tank of a 4x4 rocketed backwards out of a parking slot and rammed straight into the car in the next row. The driver climbed down from her beast, saw me and sheepishly explained that her foot was still numb from wearing her high heeled shoes on an eight-hour flight, and she had missed the brake pedal.

'Still,' she said, inspecting the back of *her* car, 'doesn't look too bad.'

'No,' I said, 'pretty good really. Pity about the other car.'

Its bumper surround was hanging off and the left light fitting was shattered.

'Well, they'll be able to fix it on insurance won't they?' she said matter of factly, as if this sort of thing occurred regularly.

Maybe it did.

Sleep, Sleep

All commercial aviation around the world works to a common timeframe known as Coordinated Universal Time or UTC (why not CUT?...well, it's a French thing). It is effectively the successor to Greenwich Mean Time (GMT). It makes sense for a global industry with a worldwide, twenty-four hours a day operation, spanning all time zones on the planet, to have a common frame of reference. Consequently, all our rosters, meteorology forecasts, flight plan data, airport information times, air traffic control (ATC) slot times, and indeed all clocks on the flight deck, are referenced to UTC.

We only deviate from this reference when trying to make sense of our constantly changing circadian (biological) clock. Although circadian body clock rhythms are self-sustaining, they are tweaked and anchored to the local environment by external cues called 'zeitgebers' (German for time giver). They include light, temperature and indeed the flow of the world around us. In effect these 'zeitgebers' synchronise the body's natural rhythm to its time zone, and if the time zone changes, they gradually shift the body clock to re-synchronise it to the new environment.

In a busy month, pilots' body clocks can be thrown through multiple time zones, from Tokyo (+nine hours) to San Francisco (- eight hours), Delhi (+five and a half hours) and then Bangkok (+eight hours). Add to that a night out of bed every time we fly, and our biological rhythms are

33

often in turmoil. There is an involved and fairly complex document that attempts to rationalise and then calculate how our body clocks change and adjust to this constant turbulence. It talks about whether a crew member is 'acclimatised', meaning 'a state in which a crew member's circadian biological clock is synchronised to the time zone where the crew member is', or whether a crew member is in an unknown state of acclimatisation.

It then lays down rules on how long our working day can be, how much rest we need between flights and whether we need extra pilots and inflight rest facilities. It works in so much as it keeps you, the flying public safe, but I have to admit that most of the time I existed in a twilight, body-clock pummelled world.

I was either coping with a large time change outbound and trying to sleep in a hotel when I was tired but everyone else around me was up-and-at-it and wouldn't let me sleep. Or I was trying to sleep when I wasn't tired because I needed some pre-flight rest, or I'd missed sleep altogether by flying through the night. Then I'd have to try and force my body into a normal home routine for a few days before it all started again.

Sleep experts will say that for a body to be healthy, it needs quality sleep. To achieve quality sleep it needs a routine, a set bedtime, and a cool, quiet, dark environment with familiar surroundings, like the same bed and pillow. And for thirty years I had none of that. For me, sleep was the single biggest challenge of my career and I have never really mastered what a lot people take for granted - the simple act of going to bed and sleeping. One of the most common flight crew phrases on seeing each other at pick-up time is 'did you sleep?'

It sometimes becomes all-consuming and the quest for sleep can rule every part of pilots' lives. I'll often talk about 'body time' meaning how my body is feeling, independent of where I am in the world and it's often in total conflict with the world in which it finds itself. I enjoyed pretty much every aspect of my job, except for the sleep element and the constant battle to get it.

Doing Their Best

Another US city and another hotel. And to be honest the hotel was not great. It was extremely dated and in desperate need of a revamp. The reception staff had done their best by giving each of the crew a suite with bedroom, living room, kitchen and two bathrooms.

Trouble was, the windows didn't fit properly, inviting the cacophony of the city into the rooms. Along every corridor, the entrance doors had swollen, making them too big for their frames meaning guests had to bang them shut repeatedly. And my bedroom was next to the service elevator. I could hear it laboriously and dejectedly scraping up and down the lift-shaft from floor to floor, followed by the sound of someone manhandling goodness knows what into or out of the lift.

Finally, at four in the morning, desperate for some sleep I grabbed my mattress and hauled it into the kitchen. Sleeping on the floor meant being perilously close to the inevitable infestation of cockroaches but if I slept with my mouth closed, I figured I would be okay. At least it was quiet.

Time Will Tell

Not so very long ago, there was a simpler and more innocent time when we flew everywhere with either the flight deck door unlocked or actually fastened open. Passengers would drift by and look in to see what was going on, and sometimes we would invite them to sit with us for take-off or landing. It was a period when my family could travel 'up front' with me, and I was able to treat my father to the full flight-deck experience from London to Geneva for his sixtieth birthday.

It was during this time that a young lad asked if he could visit the flight deck. Younger visitors are often awestruck by the sheer number of dials and buttons. Not knowing what to say, they leave us to do all the talking. That's not a criticism. If I was invited to take a look at Lewis Hamilton's Formula One car, I'd probably react in the same way, before finally saying something stupid like, 'Does it go really fast?' Anyway, this particular young man appeared to have the brain the size of a planet. He's probably supreme leader of some medium sized archipelago by now, or owns half of Wiltshire or something. His first question was, and I'm quoting here: 'What frictional effect does travelling at 500mph have on the temperature of the aircraft skin?'

Wow, I wasn't ready for that one.

Normally, if I was asked a question, it would be, 'What's that for?' And before I had managed to reply, 'Well, it's used for -', the little mite would have spotted something bigger or shinier and repeated, 'What's that for?'

And so it would go on, with me firing out a blistering salvo of replies. It was like some daemonic 'against the clock' Christmas game where you have to name as many species of deciduous trees as you can in under a minute.

'And what's that for?'

'It makes us go faster'... 'radio' ... 'shows weather' ... 'height'.

To the parent loitering in the background, I must have sounded like a crazed halfwit.

Anyway, back to the young visitor and his surprising question on friction. On the premise that it is better to show than tell, I delved into the flight management computers and pointed out that while the actual outside air temperature was -56°C, the aircraft skin was at -36°C. Which showed that the aircraft was being heated up by 20 degrees, both by friction, and the air being compressed as the aircraft punched through it. He seemed happy with that.

He then wanted to know if Einstein's theories of relativity would have an effect on his age during the flight.

37

I was tempted to say that it had obviously aged him about ten years because what sort of a question was that for a twelve-year-old to ask. Instead, I said, 'Err, err, would you like a sticker, it says *I've visited the flight deck*. You can have a postcard of the aircraft too if you like. I'll sign it?'

After he had left and the flight deck IQ levels returned to 'average', his question got me thinking. After a career amassing over 18,000 flying hours, many of which were spent at high altitudes and around 500mph, how much had my age changed according to Einstein? It seems there are two factors at work here involving both the special and general theories of relativity. The first is that the faster a traveller goes in relation to a stationary ground observer, the slower that traveller's time passes.

And it's been demonstrated as being correct, that time *slows down* for a faster moving object. Conversely the further away from a gravitational source the traveller is, like the aeroplane being six miles above the earth, then the *faster* the time will pass. They don't quite cancel each other out, and having done the maths it turns out that after a lifetime of tooling around the skies, I'm around 50 microseconds (50 millionths of a second) older than if I hadn't travelled at all.

That was all fairly pointless I hear you say. And I agree with you. Except the next time a young genius asks me that question I'll be able to answer them, and avoid the humiliation of them declining my sticker with a patronising shake of their head.

Of course, there are real-world and meaningful applications to these calculations. For example, they are used to correct the atomic clocks on the global positioning satellites we rely on so heavily these days. Nanosecond (billionth of a second) accuracy is required for dependable calculations. Without engineers understanding how much time is dilated by relativity and correcting it, satellite born clocks and the navigational data they are providing would become utterly useless in a very short period of time.

What these phenomenally clever engineers can't allow for is the carelessness of the end user. In 2008 a driver, following the directions of his SatNav, drove 145 miles north to Stamford Bridge, Yorkshire rather than 85 miles south to Stamford Bridge, home of Chelsea football club.

The Stuff of Legend

You know you're getting on a bit when you start having more and more of those "I remember when" moments.

But in fact I could tell tales of the infamous Hong Kong checkerboard approach to many a young or old pilot when I was still quite young. Hong Kong's Kai Tak airport closed in 1998 when I was still only in my late thirties, consigning it to the legends of the past.

In 1922, businessmen Ho Kai and Au Tak started a land reclamation project in Kowloon Harbour with the intention of developing the area for housing. However, shortly after the project began they went bankrupt. The work was taken over by the government but instead of creating housing they built an airport. Opened in 1925 it was dedicated to the two original entrepreneurs, and named Kai Tak Airport. After the war and several expansion projects later, it became known as Hong Kong International Airport Kai Tak.

Quite how much the original governmental department spent on the feasibility study for the long-term operation of the airport is uncertain but it can't have been more than a couple of Yuan (20p), because the single runway, orientated south east - north west, jutted out into the sea and had water on three sides. To the Northwest, there were mountains over 2000 feet high and, as time went on, the growing suburb of Kowloon's apartment blocks loomed over the perimeter fence.

With the prevailing south easterly winds, aircraft could not simply execute a straight in, stable approach to the south easterly runway. The high mountains and buildings prevented the approaching aircraft from losing sufficient height in time to reach the runway.

The word 'workaround' is not something usually associated with the aviation industry, but nevertheless that's what seems to have happened. The infamous chequerboard approach was born. It was so technically challenging that special certification was required before pilots were allowed to fly it.

Aircraft would descend out in the west, over Victoria Harbour, from 6000 feet to 2500 feet on an assisted instrument approach. After that, the autopilot had to be disconnected and the remainder of the approach was flown manually, testing the pure handling skills of even the most experienced pilot. Initially the descent would be straight towards a hill in Kowloon Thai Park. At the top of the hill, painted onto a near vertical concrete façade, was a large orange and white chequerboard pattern. This chequerboard was used as a visual reference to guide aircraft towards the point where the pilot needed to make a 47° visual right descending turn.

Typically, the plane would enter this right turn at a height of about 600 feet (50 seconds before touchdown) and exit it at around 140 feet. The start of the turn was left entirely to the judgment of the pilot who had to take into account wind speed and direction, required rate of descent and the rate of turn of a large transport aircraft when agility and manoeuvrability were not its strongest attributes.

This latter point was important as most commercial pilots would not have any experience of carrying out such a break neck manoeuvre so close to the ground. Adding to its complexity was the fact that head winds before the turn would become cross winds after the turn, resulting in the need to crab the aircraft into wind to maintain the runway centre line. All of which had to be resolved with only twenty seconds or so before touchdown. There was very little room for error and it was an extremely demanding manoeuvre.

Towards the end of its operations, the airport was handling nearly thirty million passengers per year, and using this single runway meant fine choreography to accommodate both arriving and departing aircraft. It was normal for arriving pilots who, having just negotiated the approach successfully, to be faced with an aircraft still rolling down the runway for departure.

For many airline passengers using this runway approach it became known as the Kai Tak Heart Attack. From the perspective of the passenger cabin, it was a white-knuckle ride, and very disconcerting to be banking at such close proximity to the ground, and to the city's buildings. The turn was so low, it was said passengers sitting on the right-hand side of the aircraft could actually see the television screens in people's homes.

For an observer on the ground, watching large aircraft banking so low and making such large crab angles during the final approach made for spectacular viewing and it became very popular with plane spotters.

I was lucky enough to have made three checkerboard approaches and they have got to be some of the most adrenaline fuelled, professionally satisfying events of my career.

And Goodbye

Overheard on the radio recently in the Far East:

ATC: 'Callsign 123, you are cleared to leave our zone. Contact the next sector on 124.35.'

Aircraft: 'Roger control, thank you. And before I go, could I say that this is my last flight before I retire, and in my 35 years of airline flying you are the second-best air traffic control I know.'

ATC: 'Well that's great to know, thank you. By the way, who's the best?'

Aircraft: 'Well, everybody else.'

Rude.

Through the Eyes of a Child

As the years went by, I wasn't only absent at Christmas, but also for family birthdays, weddings and christenings. In fact, I was away *a lot*. And when I was home I existed in a twilight world of jet lag and exhaustion, only really coming round in time to fly off again.

Each month, pilots in our airline would bid for pre populated lines of work which covered a four-week period, thus enabling us to have some semblance of control and stability in our lives. In reality, these 'lines' were allocated on a strict seniority basis with no flexibility for special occasions whatsoever. Of course, as a relative newbie in a very large pilot workforce I was right down the bottom of the heap, and rarely if ever got the days off I wanted. Consequently, Pen became adept (and not a little frustrated) at holding the fort, and attending events on her own with our small children in tow.

We did our best to keep the children in the loop on where Daddy was in the world by showing them photos I'd taken on my travels (it was before the days of Instagram, Zoom and FaceTime).

Pen remembers driving past the tall skyscraper-like building on the outskirts of Basingstoke which once housed the 'AA' (Automobile Association, not Alcoholics Anonymous). Our two-year-old son James pointed at the building from his car seat and proudly pronounced, 'Kong Kong!' He had obviously taken a keen interest in my photos of soaring skyscrapers from my latest trip to Hong Kong!

A year later, having returned from yet another lengthy trip, Pen was relaying a conversation she had had with James.

Apparently, he had said, 'I know Daddy is away again.'

'How do you know he's away?' Pen asked.

'Because his head is missing.'

After further quizzing, it turned out that to my three-year-old son, Daddy was either a head sticking out of the duvet, fast asleep, or it was missing altogether because he was at work.

It was time for a change. I sincerely hoped it would be a change for the better, a chance to see more of my family, but I was in for a nasty shock.

1995-2000
Airbus, First Officer

The short-haul Airbus fleet, used exclusively on the internal and European network, includes the A318, A319, A320 and A321. They are all short to medium range, single aisle, twin engine jet airliners that can accommodate 107 to 236 passengers and have a range of 3,500 to 4,300 miles, depending on model.

The Airbus A320 family of aircraft was the first group of commercial airliners to feature a full glass cockpit and digital fly-by-wire (FBW) flight control system. The glass cockpit features LCD multi-functional flight instrument displays rather than the traditional style of analogue dials and gauges. FBW replaces the conventional, heavy, manual flight controls of pulleys, cranks and tension cables with a computer interpreted and electrically signalled control system. Pilot-operated side-sticks are used to control the aircraft.

Madness in Madrid

The international language of aviation is English, which is a good thing because my grasp of other languages is worse than a pre-school child and I'm inclined to make stuff up. Once, when about to go horse riding in Scandinavia I asked if it was time to 'scrumble up di beastie'. There is an exception to the rule: pilots flying in their own country are allowed the option of speaking in their native tongue. This doesn't happen very often at busy international airports because it means non-native speakers are unable to build up a picture of what is going on around them.

We were flying into Madrid. The airport is 2000 feet above sea level and summer time temperatures regularly reach 30°C, so it was definitely in the 'hot and high' airport category. Energy management and speed control would be paramount. With that taken into account, we were on the final approach course, at final approach speed, all ready to land.

We then heard a conversation between the controller and another aircraft. It was in Spanish, and I couldn't understand a word of it. Soon afterwards a small turboprop aircraft approached at high speed from our right-hand side. He banked sharply and ended up on the same approach path about two miles ahead of us, effectively jumping the queue to land. This was highly unusual because aircraft on final approach need stable and known separation from other traffic. And this particular manoeuvre seemed especially misjudged.

We were now very close to the turboprop – a situation which should have been totally unacceptable to both the air traffic controller and the pilots of the turboprop. In executing this queue-jumping manoeuvre, they were now way too fast and needed to reduce from their 'attack speed' down to a reasonable final approach speed. I saw that the landing gear was lowered, speed breaks deployed and landing flaps thrown out, all in a desperate attempt to increase drag and slow down. I could imagine the fury of hands flashing around the flight deck and the result must have been quite disconcerting for their passengers.

In comparison to our Airbus, the turboprop was a much smaller aircraft and had a slower final approach speed, and we were now catching them up. To register our concern with air traffic control we asked pointedly if we were still cleared for our approach.

No answer.

Instead, we heard more Spanish, but this time at a higher pitch and with more urgency. Again, I couldn't understand what was being said, but I imagine it was something like:

'Jesus Christ, Juan, the British are catching you up, you must land. Land!'

Meanwhile we reassessed our position and agreed that if things became too close for comfort, we would execute a go around for another approach*. But for the time being, we were happy to sit and watch events unfold.

I suspect the turboprop crew were now regretting their actions, as this self-imposed stress would surely be taking years off their otherwise mañana driven lives. They hit the runway in a blaze of burning rubber and, trying to control extreme braking, swerved drastically from right to left as if wrestling with a rally car. We watched the drama with incredulous fascination.

We were quite close to the runway now, and started rehearsing the go around.

More Spanish from the air traffic controller, possibly along the lines of: 'For the love of God, Juan, get off the runway. Get off!'

Shortly afterwards, the turboprop ricocheted off the runway and down a high-speed taxiway. I imagined the poor passengers screaming like roller coaster captives.

A few minutes later the controller finally switched back to English: 'Er, British sorry, er, cleared to land. Sorry.'

I had never seen the like of it before and, thankfully, I have never seen anything like it since.

The captain and I are good friends and because of this, he was apt to push his luck with me. He would often sign off his 'goodbye PA' with the words, 'and finally, ladies and gentlemen, my first officer will sing to you'.

But, we were both pretty frazzled and so after we had closed down the engines, I turned to him and said, 'no singing today'.

He let me off the hook that time.

*A 'go around' is designed to get a landing aircraft safely back into the air. They can be ordered by either air-traffic control or initiated by the pilots and are necessary if it's deemed unsafe to land. There are several reasons why a 'go around' might be carried out; the most common being if the runway has something on it, like a preceding aircraft. It is a very precise manoeuvre requiring the pilots to follow a specific published route and adhere to set height and speed restrictions, whilst reconfiguring the aircraft from a landing set up to a take-off one, and at the same time liaising with air traffic control.

Every runway in the world has its own individual and specific 'go around' pattern designed to avoid physical dangers such as surrounding high ground, other aircraft routes, and special airspace. There are patterns designed to avoid the disturbance caused by flying over city centres, as well as more indulgent ones: I know of a prince who has banned aircraft from flying over his palace. Fair do's I suppose; it's his country.

As you can imagine, it is a busy time for the pilots, which is why you might not hear from them for a minute or two after a 'go around'. We understand that it can be very disconcerting for a passenger who, having expected to land, is suddenly shot skywards again.

But, be assured it is something we practice in every six-monthly simulator test, usually with an engine failure thrown in for good measure, in the worst weather conditions, and without the help of the autopilot.

Bouncing Around Europe

As I settled into the short-haul routine, it quickly became apparent that whilst there was no jet-lag there were still plenty of sleepless nights. 'Earlies' meant a 3:00 am start to allow time to travel to the airport, briefings and pre-flight checks for a 6:00 am flight.

Trips were rarely 'there and back and go home'. Instead, they were all stacked together, sometime into five-day tours. In those five days, we could fly eighteen sectors, bouncing around Europe and ending each evening in a different city and a different hotel. Our down-route off-duty time was just long enough to have a meal and a beer and go to bed. It was groundhog days on 'earlies'.

So much for my vain hope of spending more time at home with my family.

Keeping Fit

We had a brand-new system of receiving allowances during our stop-overs. It meant approaching the hotel reception staff, identifying ourselves as crew and, when challenged, providing two characters of our password. They would then give us local currency up to a maximum daily limit. The great advantage of this was at the end of the stay we could hand back any unused currency, which meant we didn't have vast quantities of local shrapnel or unspendable local *scroots* to carry around. The balance was converted to sterling and deducted from our salary.

I used the system for the first time in Jersey. At the time, the crew hotel there was a grand, elegant place with a classic French chateau facade. It exuded early 1900s sophistication and had a workforce to match. The reception staff behaved like characters in a 1920s novel. They would talk to you deferentially whilst at the same time giving the impression you smelled like a particularly odious, overripe piece of cheese. They also had a way of answering questions whilst making you feel totally unworthy.... of everything. I loved bantering with them as they always remained deadpan and never missed a beat. It was great fun.

I approached the receptionist who was staring intently at a computer screen. His name tag identified him as John.

'What ho, John, tip top day, what,' I said, hoping my banter was of the period.

After ignoring me for an uncomfortably long time which masterfully fell just short of rude, he raised his head from the screen and said, 'Yes sir, it seems the recent inclement weather has ceased for the time being'.

I said, 'Rather! Was wondering if I could grab some local denarii from you'.

This was met with a stony-faced stare, so I sheepishly changed tack:

'Please could I take out some crew allowances?'

'Very good, sir. If you would kindly wait while I summon my colleague who deals with that sort of thing,' he replied with a barely suppressed sneer on his lips.

Dealing with petty cash was obviously completely beneath him. Whilst I waited for his colleague, a middle-aged lady dressed in what looked like tennis whites from the 1950s, complete with tinted sun visor, approached at speed.

'I need to go to the gym,' she panted in an American accent.

It sounded to me like some sort of keep fit emergency.

'Indeed, madam,' said John.

'What? Do you think I need to go to the gym?'

'No madam, I was just acknowledging your desire to attend the gymnasium.'

'Okay, so where is it.'

'Where is what, madam?'

'The gym, where is the gym?'

'The gymnasium is there, madam, just outside and on the other side of the entrance portico. One can observe the word gymnasium emblazoned on the wall.' He pointed to a building not even a stone's throw away.

'And how do I get there?'

'I'm sorry madam, I don't understand your question.'

'I mean, have I got to walk?'

'I'm afraid so, but perhaps madam could incorporate the thirty-foot journey into her exercise routine in order to mitigate the ordeal. If you set off now it could all be over within a matter of moments.'

'I've never heard anything so ridiculous in my life,' she huffed.

'I concur entirely, madam,' he replied, steeling the slightest of sideways glances at me. After a moment, he added, 'Ah, sir, here is my colleague who I am sure will be delighted to furnish you with the requisite funding. And, madam, if you require any further assistance, please address your queries to him directly.'

And with that, he returned to staring at the computer monitor as if nothing had happened and no one was there.

Port in the port of Porto

We were on the ground in Porto, Portugal, with a fifty minute turnaround before heading back to London. Having prepared the aircraft for the return flight we decided to have our crew meal. Eating a meal on short-haul was always the same, and involved attacking a few morsels of food served in a foil tray with the gusto of a half-starved wild dog. It was not a pretty sight, but made necessary due to constant time pressures. More so that day because the captain wanted to go into the terminal building to buy some port.

The meal devoured and indigestion assured, he set off at speed towards the terminal building, arriving back ten minutes later with a broad smile on his face. With no time for him to tell his story, we boarded our passengers and set off for London. Once in the cruise when things had settled down, he reached into his flight bag and brought out his prize. 'What do you think of this,' he said with obvious pride. 'It's a thirty-year-old bottle of vintage port.'

'It looks very nice. It's got dust on it and everything,' I said.

'Yes, and very cheap. It was only 40,000 escudos, which is about £14. Ridiculous,' he said.

'Oh.'

'What?'

'Nothing.'

'Don't be jealous, you said you didn't want anything.'

'No, it's not that,' I said. 'I think in your rush to buy the port you got the decimal point wrong. That's a £140 bottle you have there.'

Like a chameleon, he started to turn the same colour as his lovely vintage port.

Vegetarians Look Away Now

Lyon has a reputation as one of the gastronomic centres of France. And as France quite fancies itself with regard to food, our expectations were high.

The captain and I walked around town and spotted a restaurant brimming with clientele. We thought that was a good sign, and so with my best franglais asked for 'un table pour deux por favor.' The maître d's lips curled into a snarl of contempt. Begrudgingly, he led us to a table that probably had the best view of the toilets in the whole restaurant. He then handed us menus as though we were lepers and skulked off. We stared at them crestfallen. There were no handy translations so we asked a waiter if there was an English menu available. He simply said 'non' and walked away. It seemed we were on our own.

We both made a stab at ordering, by pointing at the menu which did nothing for the mood of the waiter, who looked as if he was thinking 'ignorant foreigners'. Eventually our food arrived, and, oh my goodness. Mine was a plate of five anaemic boiled potatoes and what appeared to be a schnitzel. Well, it had breadcrumbs on it.

The captain had evidently ordered pig's trotter because that's what was standing on his plate. Literally a pig's foot with hooves, and I swear there was still mud between its toes. As a way of varying the accompanying vegetables, his meal came with four boiled potatoes. No sauce that the French are supposedly famous for. He stared at his plate for a moment and then, with what could only be described as heroic determination, poked the foot with his knife and fork, only to find the rubbery skin resisted his advances. He tried harder but only succeeded in pushing it off his plate and onto the floor.

Amazingly it landed the right way up. We both watched, wide eyed, as it continued its grease-assisted journey across the floor towards the next table, like some grotesque horror movie clip from 'Revenge of the pigs'. I quickly hooked it back with my foot and pulled it out of sight under our table.

I said he could share my schnitzel. I cut into it to reveal something pale and slimy. I'm not squeamish. I'd resorted to eating all sorts of weird things including worms and slugs on a military survival exercise some years before, so I thought I would be brave and try a piece. I spent the next five minutes dry heaving into my napkin. We didn't know it at the time but apparently my order, 'les poumons, le mou,' translates as 'slack ox lung' or something. I can tell you we were having a really offal time of it, unlike the other diners who were all eagerly chowing down on all manner of monstrous food. Presumably they were trying to outdo each other by eating the most disgusting thing on the menu. I half expected a bell to ring and a proud diner to stand up and take a bow because he'd managed to gag down his plate full of horse foreskin.

And then someone else would say, 'I've heard the pig scrotum is particularly good here'.

'Yes, but not as good as the fricassee of goats' eyelid.'

I've probably just made those two up. Or maybe not, because later I looked up other delicious French offal recipes and found 'tetines' (cows' udders), 'le rognon blanc, les animelles' (testicles), and 'Ris de veax' (calves' pancreas).

So, we feasted on our dry boiled potatoes but I left the lung gasping on the side of the plate and the captain's hoof under the table. When the waiter came back to check on progress, he looked happily at the captain's empty plate. By rights there should have been at least a few discarded tendons, gristle and toe nails. Clearly this man before him was a master 'offal-ateer.'

I could see he was considering ringing the bell but then he glanced across at me, and his face dropped. Suddenly I was the son who had brought shame and disappointment on his father. 'You did not like it?' he asked, eyeing the car crash that was my plate.

He was talking to someone from the UK. And as you know, most Brits can go into any restaurant, bitch and moan about the table, the prices, the service and the food, and then when asked if everything was okay, we immediately chime, 'yes, very nice, thank you'. And that's what I gave him, with both barrels. To make the point I rubbed my stomach and blew air out of puffed cheeks to indicate I couldn't eat another thing.

He did the famous Gallic shrug, and I knew he was thinking 'lying, weak stomached, little shit,' as he slinked off to get the bill. It came with four mint imperials. We pounced on them with unseemly haste, and were surprised and delighted to discover they were actually mints and not kidney stones from a sickly goat. We thought £20 a head seemed entirely reasonable, because the potatoes had been boiled very well.

After the ordeal we went to a pub to drown our sorrows and to be honest we rather over did it because when we came out, we couldn't remember where we were, or how to get back to the hotel. We staggered around and eventually found a taxi. I always carry a hotel card in my back pocket for just such emergencies. I handed it to the taxi driver, who read it and then remonstrated loudly and pointed for us to get out of his taxi. Frankly, I'd had just about enough of the whole evening and was in no mood for this. I waved my hand irritably at the card and gestured for him to get on with it. He continued to gesticulate and said something forceful in French. I countered by sitting back and folding my arms like a petulant child. He eventually shrugged his shoulders, started the engine, drove around the corner and stopped again.

Now what?

We followed his pointing finger and then we both started rolling around the back seat, laughing like a couple of three-year-olds being tickled. We were outside the entrance to our hotel.

The next day for lunch I decided to cock a snoot at this gastronomic centre by going to a famous fast-food restaurant. Same mashed up animal products, but I felt as if I had dined like a king.

Bravo

Many English letters sound very similar (b and d, s and f, m and n) and they can be easily misheard when communicating on a radio. Lack of face-to-face visual cues, loud background noise, radio static or interference all add to the possible confusion. Misheard letters are merely annoying when trying to give your postcode or email address to someone over the phone but they could have fatal consequences in a safety critical environment like aviation.

For example, it's not always necessary to take-off using the full length of a runway. Providing the aircraft's performance allows it and the correct calculations are made, it may ease traffic congestion, be more convenient or simply quicker to use an intermediate point (called an intersection) further along the runway. These intermediate points are usually denoted by a letter. Intersection A is at the full length. Shorter take-off distances would be designated points B, C, D and so on. It's easy to see the catastrophic consequences of being told to use intersection B but you heard and used intersection D, a much shorter distance.

To avoid this problem, we use a phonetic alphabet. In the past, varying sets of 'phonetic alphabets' have been used by different organisations in different countries around the world. They use a series of twenty-six English-centric words to represent the twenty-six letters of the alphabet. You may remember those American cop shows of the 1970s where a car's licence plate would be read as 'Able Baker Dog 59', meaning 'ABD 59'.

But these alphabets were only intended to be used by people from not only the same nation but also the same organisation, and confusion arose when they were employed in a global operation like aviation. Edward, Easy, Echo and Emil are just four of the phonetic words used around the world to denote the letter E.

To bring order out of this muddle, a standardised phonetic alphabet was introduced by ICAO (International Civil Aviation Organization) and has been the spelling standard for virtually all national and international organisations since the 1960s. In order to choose the twenty-six code words for the letters, hundreds of comprehension tests were carried out to discover which words were the easiest to understand over voice communication by volunteers from thirty-one nations, heard not only in isolation but in the context of a message. For example: Bravo was chosen for B, Foxtrot for F and Zulu for Z.

Some slight tweaking was necessary in order to help non-English speaking students learn the correct pronunciation. A is Alpha, but is spelt Alfa as the 'ph' sound is not recognised internationally, and could well have resulted in it being pronounced 'alp-ha'. J is Juliett, but is spelt Juliet to avoid the possibility of French speakers pronouncing it 'joo-lee-ay.'

The only anomaly I have come across is for the letter D, which is normally pronounced Delta. However, Atlanta International Airport is the operating hub for Delta airlines. To avoid the confusion of so many Deltas being bandied about, the airport authority have re-classified D as Dixie. It avoids confusion so long as you manage to see the tiny note tucked away on one of the charts explaining the change. I've often heard pilots say, 'Taxiway Dixie? What the hell is he talking about?'

The adoption of the standardised phonetic alphabet meant differences in accent, language and pronunciation was no longer a problem, and it is a great achievement. Apart from at Atlanta, I have only ever heard it cause confusion once, and that was not ICAO's fault.

Having landed at Paris Charles de Gaulle Airport we heard another pilot, who clearly thought he was a wag and a wit, report: 'De Gaulle ground [control] we have come to a halt as there is a fox trotting along taxiway Foxtrot.' Confused, the French ground controller said, 'I don't understand this word *trotting*. What is the fox doing?'

'Well, I'd like to say that the fox trotting along taxiway Foxtrot was doing the foxtrot, but if you really want to know, it is now having a shit.'

As quick as you like, the controller replied, 'Er, OK. Give it some privacy, and when it is finished, you may proceed'.

We were impressed not only with the controller's typically French cheeky sense of humour, but also the fact there was at least one Frenchman who could relate to the issue of privacy with regard to toiletry functions.

Beyond the Pale

Robin was a cabin manager. She was a lovely person and, having flown with her several times, I knew her well. She seemed upset and I asked her what was wrong. She said there had been a crisis at home and she had needed to speak to her husband. She had called our operation centre, explaining that her husband was one of the crew presently on a trip in Cape Town. It was pre iPhone days, and she needed the hotel's details so she could contact him. They gave her the number of the hotel, but added she was unlikely to get hold of him. According to their records, he was currently on a week's leave.

'That can't be possible. I helped him pack his suitcase and he left home in his uniform three days ago.'

It turned out he was having an affair. He had pretended to go to work but instead had taken a romantic break with his mistress. And he had used one of their precious week's leave in the bargain.

It's Sauna the Same to Me

It was a fairly cold and miserable day in Hamburg. I decided to use the hotel's health spa and go for a relaxing sauna. After showering, clad in just my 'swimmies' and armed with a towel, I pulled open the sauna door to be confronted with a naked, blonde, German lady, spread eagled on the top rotisserie. Panicking and acutely embarrassed by all that exposed flesh, and feeling foolish I hadn't noticed the sign telling me I had walked into the female section by mistake, I quickly closed the door. I really hoped she hadn't spotted me, because knowing my luck I'd meet her in the lift later that evening.

I went to ask the health spa receptionist to direct me to the male sauna. Apparently, it was all unisex. It would be, wouldn't it? It was Germany.

I could see from the receptionist's expression that I had stumbled across one of their national sports. Confront a Brit with something unthinkable, and watch what happens. I had a choice, and conflicting impulses flip-flopped through my brain. I could brazenly stand my ground and stare her out, and then nonchalantly walk back to that den of iniquity, or I could admit defeat and make a run for it. I dug deep and with true British bulldog spirit, I walked back to the sauna.

I crept back in as quietly as possible, hoping not to make eye contract. Or any other contact for that matter. But it was all in vain. The naked, blonde, German lady opened her eyes, lifted her head, looked me up and down and pointed at my swimming trunks. I'm guessing it was obvious I wasn't local because she said, in English, 'No'. As if to say, 'if you don't take those off, you'll be a pervert'. Which I thought was the wrong way round really.

I slid out of my trunks, gingerly holding them in front of my privates, feeling hugely uncomfortable and battling against a lifetime of social conditioning. The voice inside my head was screaming, 'this isn't right. It's going to lead to a custodial sentence for indecent exposure'.

I needed a refuge and eyed the wooden slatted bench, trying not to think of how many sweaty arses had been there before me.

I suddenly thought, 'towel! Sit on the towel like you're supposed to do'.

That was all well and good, but how could I lay out my towel whilst trying to protect my modesty? The naked, blonde lady was now looking at me like a cat trying to decide whether to continue playing with its food, or put whatever it was out of its misery. I was praying for the latter. There was nothing for it. I dropped my trunks on the floor. Whilst I struggled with my towel, and in order to fill the excruciating silence, and to break the ice, (which was a silly thing to think considering where I was), I smiled sheepishly and said, 'It's like a sauna in here'.

Being German, she agreed that of course it was like a sauna, because it was.

This was not the relaxing experience I had hoped for. I was desperate to get up and leave, and wondered what would be the minimum acceptable amount of time before I could. It turned out to be about two minutes.

Sixth Sense

I had just completed my 'essentials for command' ground course, designed to give first officers about to start their command training the basics of what was expected of an airline captain. It was taken as read that at this stage of our career, the process of flying and managing a flight was second nature. Now it was time to concentrate on the more esoteric aspects. Barristers came to speak to us about the substantial legal responsibilities of a captain and their incredibly wide-ranging legal powers (almost dictatorial in extent), plus talks on leadership and conflict resolution.

The course was run in-house by our training captains and on the whole was well-pitched and well-presented, with the exception of one captain who was clearly in love with himself, his role and his status, and loved nothing more than to talk down to us as if we were children. His attitude suggested we knew nothing, and we should be very grateful to be in receipt of his gems of wisdom.

He stressed repeatedly that as lowly first officers we probably hadn't yet developed that 'sixth sense' that *je ne sais quoi*, that 'all- knowing, all-seeing godliness' of a senior captain - but it would come with time. I thought he came across as a bit of a 'know-it-all'.

Anyway, fast forward a week and I was now in Jersey, about to fly the return trip to London. We could hear a radio conversation between one of our B757's and ground control. It seemed the pilots of the B757 has ventured down a taxiway that was too small for them. They were now boxed in and had nowhere to turn around. In the words of A. A. Milne and Winnie the Pooh, they were 'stuck in a great tightness'.

In response to a comment from the 757 captain that they hadn't been told about the size restriction, the ground controller calmly pointed out that there was a note on the charts. It had also been highlighted in the airfield notices and there was a ruddy great sign by the taxiway entrance!

And best of all, the captain's voice was unmistakable. It was the smug, all-knowing training captain from the previous week.

Today is the Day

Having achieved the seniority to apply for a command, and successfully passed the simulator and route flying phases, this was the day of days, my final command check. If I passed, I would hopefully reach another milestone in my career, and finally become a captain.

You will be relieved to know they don't make it easy to pass this exam, and many don't first time around, with a few never passing it, ever. The command check is a normal commercial flight during which we have to demonstrate excellence in everything. And I had been rostered Madrid. Thanks to my earlier experiences of Madrid, I would have much preferred flying to, well, anywhere else.

I had spent the previous evening examining the charts in minute detail: The arrival routes over the Sistema Central Mountain range; the subtleties of each runway and the complex ground taxi routes; identifying pitfalls and dangers. I reasoned it was too late to learn Spanish. I'd just have to wing it on that score.

The next day I arrived at the report centre primed and ready. I could have appeared on Mastermind with my specialist subject, 'Madrid Air Traffic controllers and their particular foibles,' and I think I would have put in a half-decent performance. I was greeted by the fleet pilot manager, who was also going to be the examiner.

He informed me the flight had been cancelled! Not to worry, he would commandeer another flight so my command check could go ahead, but it would be a fairly last-minute thing. So much for being able to plan ahead. I went to inform the 'co-pilot' who was doing the flight with me. For this exam the co-pilot is always a very experienced training captain. His brief was to act as a 'competent co-pilot but lacking initiative.' In reality this meant he would demonstrate excellence in blinking and keeping his seat warm but unless asked to do something, he would do nothing. He had to be told exactly what to do and when to do it. If his errors were not spotted and corrected in time, and if events had the potential to become complicated, needing him to *actually* demonstrate initiative, I would fail.

A couple of hours later the flight manager arrived, beaming. He had found a flight for me: Manchester. Great news in many ways as I would remain tucked up inside the UK. It was very busy airspace but I would be looked after by, in my view, some of the best air-traffic controllers in the world. However, the straight-line distance from London to Manchester is only 130 miles with a flight time of around thirty-five minutes.

For fuel efficiency these flights are often planned with the trajectory of a cannonball. A climb section followed immediately by a descent with no level cruise. The cruise part of a flight is normally used for regrouping, planning the arrival and briefing. Time management would be one of the most crucial parts of this flight.

A pre-flight aircraft is like a hungry chick, with a seemingly insatiable appetite. On the flight deck there are around 400 primary use switches, most with multifunction options and each one has, obviously, to be set up correctly.

Flight computers need inputting with the route, expected aircraft weight, and environmental data to allow the correct calculation of take-off speeds, flap settings, engine power, climb speeds and cruise altitudes.

On top of this, there is a constant stream of people entering the flight deck demanding the captain's attention and authorisation. Coordinators wanting to discuss passenger boarding, cargo details and special loads; refuellers discussing fuel requirements; caterers; engineers discussing minor issues and rectifications, and the crew with a myriad of other queries. It's a mental juggling act needing the highest level of discipline to accommodate these interruptions, resolve issues and then pick up from where you personally left off.

And all the while, the co-pilot/training captain in the other seat was sitting there, glassy-eyed, staring blankly out of the window. He was really getting into his role with gusto. I half expected to see his eyes roll up in their sockets. I resolved to treat him like some organic 'to-do' list, and push on.

I did manage to complete everything before our scheduled time of departure, but only just. I had hoped to briefly talk through the arrival procedure into Manchester, as there would be precious little time to do so in the air but unfortunately, I didn't get the chance. I decided I'd make time in the air by restricting our maximum altitude to give us a small five-minute cruise section. As we were taxiing away from the stand one of the cabin crew contacted me to say we had a very irate passenger on board. From his window seat, he had just seen his hard-shell case containing two very expensive shot guns. They should have been loaded into the hold but for some reason they had been left on the tarmac. I quickly glanced at Dave, the examiner, who refused to look up from something clearly very important in his note book. I glanced at John, the co-pilot/training captain who continued to stare blankly ahead.

'Okay John,' I said. 'Options. We can either go back to stand, but that would mean missing our take-off slot and possibly incurring a long delay whilst we organise the guns to be loaded. Or we can carry on and call operations and have them loaded onto the next flight. What do you think?'

'Great idea,' said John cheerfully.

'Which one?'

'Both, of course.'

'OK, great thanks for that, very useful. Call ops and have them send the guns on, will you.'

The flight progressed well with no further hitches. I treated John as if he was an idiot and he obliged by behaving like one, but that was fine. We knew the game and we were both playing it as best we could. Predictably in the descent, John let the aircraft get high on the ideal descent profile.

'We are getting a little high John,' I said.

'Yes,' he replied.

I looked at him and once again he was staring vacantly out of the window with a silly half-grin on his face. 'Increase the rate of descent John,' I said in a weary tone that conveyed I wouldn't let him get away with anything.

'OK,' he said with a slight smile as if to say, '*enough is enough*.' He started behaving like a real person after that.

Once on the ground I had just enough time to savage my crew meal before preparing for the return flight. The ground coordinator came onto the flight deck holding what looked like a soft sided insulated picnic box.

'Where do you want me to put this?' he asked.

'What is it?' I asked.

'It's living human flesh. It's going to one of the London hospitals for transplant.'

At this, Dave the examiner's ears pricked up. I could see him thinking, 'what is he going to do about this?'

I thought, 'what am I going to do about this?'

I glanced at the library that all aircraft carry, consisting of twenty or so books, each between three and four centimetres thick. They make up our operations manual. Effectively the law on how we should operate our aircraft. I grabbed a couple of them and started scanning the indices for obvious hints on what to do: 'transplant', 'human flesh', 'weird zombie shit'.

It soon became apparent there was nothing written down. I made the decision to take the bag onto the flight deck for safekeeping, having established that it had been scanned through security first.

Back at Heathrow and in the debriefing room Dave said, 'It just goes to show that no matter how much you legislate and formalise proceedings, a captain will often have to make decisions based on the available information and experience, and come up with the best possible plan. And as you are now a captain you can start to build that experience. Congratulations'.

2000-2003
Airbus 319/20/21, Captain

There are rules, equations and laws that can be used to describe the workings of the physical world around us, and in particular the world of flight. For example, Newton's third law of motion states that, 'For every action there is an equal and opposite reaction'. This law explains why jet engines push an aeroplane through the sky.

I have my own particular rule that I've used to great effect during my years as an airline captain, especially when streamlining decision-making in times of stress.

It goes like this:

'Whilst on the flight deck, if you are handed anything, you can't go wrong if you either sign it or eat it.'

A Rum Lot

I had been in Manchester for the night (well half a night, as it was still only 4:45am). I was up, dressed in my uniform, and leaving my room for an early morning pickup to the airport. As I rounded the corner to take the lift down to reception, I came across a sight that took me by surprise. Next to the lifts there was sofa and a mock antique table bearing a softly glowing lamp. All very Homes and Gardens you might think. Except on the sofa there was a lady, totally naked, on her back, legs in the air. Filling the gap between those legs was a man, also without a stitch on, who, I think in the correct local vernacular was, 'giving her what for'.

I wasn't sure what to do so I just stood there, staring, and finally gave a polite cough. On hearing this intrusion, the guy looked up from the task at hand, and without missing a beat, as it were, asked if I could use another lift. It was said so matter of factly that all I could think of saying was, 'no problem, have a good weekend'.

Have a good weekend? What was I thinking? I tucked my captain's hat under my arm and as I headed towards the emergency exit, the lady turned her head towards me and smiled. Evidently these people were not the shy and retiring type. I came out of the emergency stairwell, one floor down, peering round the corner and hoping for something less weird - perhaps the four horsemen of the apocalypse. Mercifully, nothing. The lift arrived, the doors opened and for the second time in what was becoming an increasingly long morning, I stared.

'Ooh, 'ello love, jump in.'

A different lady but with the same indifferent attitude to her circumstances. She was in the process of getting dressed, bare feet next to stiletto boots, and she seemed to be having trouble with her 'boob tube' top.

Clearly, she had never heard of correct lift protocol of staring at the walls in silence. 'Zip me up, would you love. You a pilot then?'

'Yes,' I said. 'You a sex worker?'

No, I didn't say that last bit, but what could I say? 'Business going well? Busy weekend?' Finally, we reached the ground floor, the doors opened and we both exited. She was still chatting away as though we were great friends. The airline driver waiting for us beamed at me with a nod and a wink.

She saw him and said, 'Ooh, if you've got transport, I could do with a lift across town'.

What a lively lot they are in Manchester.

Now You See It, Now You Don't

Flying from Hamburg to Heathrow at our cruise altitude of 40,000 feet, we saw an aircraft up in our ten o'clock (that's front left) and at a much higher altitude. It was definitely a visibly solid object but too far away to make out any distinguishing shapes or features. We were bemused because it wasn't showing up on our TCAS* and it's unusual for commercial airliners to fly much higher than around 43,000 feet. Radio chatter was quiet, so out of interest we asked the controller what the aircraft was, and at what level. Maybe it was military? He replied there was nothing on his radar and that no one had a flight plan that would explain it. Nor were there any notified military activity in the area. He said maybe it was an error of our TCAS system.

We replied that it was not showing on our instruments; we were physically looking at it. The controller remained adamant that, as far as he was concerned, it wasn't there.

The UK government has recently released its Unidentified Flying Object reports from 1997 to 2009 on the Gov.UK website. Out of curiosity I had a quick look. January 2009 was a busy month for UFOs, clocking up forty-three reported sightings.

Many of them mention orange lights such as the report from an air traffic control employee in Warwickshire: 'an orange glowing object with a red light on the right-hand side.'

The report from Malvern Worcestershire on the 5th January is a bit different: 'A V shaped formation similar to how birds fly of seven lights. Moved rapidly across the sky, rotated slightly then the lights split up and vanished. The lights were the size and brightness of stars. No noise and no visible trails in the sky.'

But my favourite has to be from a member of the public on the 29th January from Colchester in Essex: 'We keep getting flown over by aliens galore. They are dropping germs and we keep getting colds. Please send the RAF or USAF to stop them.'

Now I'm not suggesting the object we saw that morning was being flown by little green men, but it *was* flying and it *was* unidentified. So, I guess we had our own UFO sighting that day. And I'm glad it was only a sighting. I understand that Area 51 conspiracists who claim to have had a UFO encounter all walk bow legged and have a powerful aversion to probe like objects.

* TCAS Traffic Alert and Collision Avoidance System. A system that shows pilots the relative position and height of other aircraft in its immediate vicinity. TCAS extrapolates the flight paths of all these aircraft and if it predicts a conflict, it will initially direct the pilots of the conflicting aircrafts to visually identify one another. If the conflict continues, it issues a command to both aircraft to take mutually avoiding action. This all happens independently of air traffic control.

'Ah-Har, Me-Hearty'

A uniform makes its wearer stand out from the crowd. You are on display. When I walked through the terminal building, I have to admit my appearance made me feel proud. I also hoped people would look at me and feel confident I could keep them safely in the air for the next eight hours or so.

One day, whilst I was wending my way through the terminal, a young boy spotted me, turned to his father and shouted, 'Look, daddy, look, there's the pirate'. I loved the idea of being a pirate - a real step up from the previous week. Admittedly, then, I was in casual clothes and waiting to pick my daughter up from school. I was fighting jet lag, I was tired and hadn't slept well the previous evening. I was feeling, and probably looked, grotty. A little four-year-old chap eyed me for a while. Then he pulled on his mother's sleeve, pointed at me, and asked, 'what's that man for?' Fair question, I thought. Right there and then I'm not sure I could have given him a good answer.

Anyway, back to being a pirate. In a (very) round-about way, it reminded me of the safety demonstration given before take-off and landing. If you have ever wondered about the reasoning behind some of the instructions given to you during that demo, here is a decode for you:

If you need to put on a life jacket, there is reason you are advised to tie a double bow. A single bow is just like your shoe lace, one tug and it pulls apart. A double bow makes it secure and it won't come undone even if accidentally grappled by another frantic passenger, meaning as you jump into the water you won't slip through the jacket and keep going down.

You are instructed to return your seat to the upright position so as to enable the passenger sitting behind you to adopt the 'brace' position if necessary.

The reason why the window blinds are always raised for take-off and landing is to give you an outside visual reference of up and down should an emergency develop. And the reason the lights are dimmed for a take-off and landing at night? That's to adjust your eyes to low light conditions should an evacuation takes place. It also makes the emergency exit lights easier to spot.

So why did a pirate remind me of all that? Well, apparently, the classic image of pirates sporting eyepatches was possibly down to the fact they were protecting one eye from the bright sunlight of the Caribbean. This ensured that when they stormed the lower decks of an enemy ship, one eye would be acclimatised to lowlight conditions. It gave them a tactical advantage.

But I'm not sure what tactical advantage they achieved from having a parrot sitting on their shoulder shouting 'pieces of eight'.

Getting Some Fresh Air

Cabin air is a mix of fresh air drawn from outside the aircraft, and recycled cabin air that has passed through extremely efficient filters. Known as High Efficiency Particulate Air (or HEPA) filters, they are capable of trapping more than 99.99% of all microscopic sized bacteria, including those that cause Covid-19.

The air, which meets hospital operating theatre standards, enters the cabin at overhead compartment level and is extracted at floor level, meaning that the air is drawn down and, importantly, not allowed to flow forward or aft along the cabin.

In normal operation, less than half the air is filtered and recirculated, the rest is fresh air drawn-in from outside. On a typical commercial aircraft, the cabin air is completely replaced every three minutes.

Air supplied to aircraft toilets, galleys and cargo-holds is not filtered, but is dumped directly overboard to avoid recycling foul smelling air.

Air supplied to the flight deck is 100% fresh air and is at a slightly higher pressure than the cabin air. This provides a small positive pressure, preventing any smoke and fumes entering the flight deck from the cabin.

I Take my Hat off to You

It was route check time again. Another exam in the yearly cycle that rolls relentlessly on.

We were rostered to fly a scheduled flight from London to Bilbao and back, accompanied by an examiner, whose role was to observe and report on our competence as professional aircrew doing our day-to-day job, and ultimately decide whether we kept our pilots' licences. In reality the examiners were our own training captains authorised by the Civil Aviation Authority. Just because they were 'in house' pilots, didn't mean they were any the less strict or uncompromising. On the plus side, we all knew each other on the fleet and so it was possible to judge whether the person looking over our shoulders for the day was a Dr Jekyll or Mr Hyde.

Our examiner for the day was Michael Actually. He was not Mike and definitely not Mick, and if anyone should call him anything other than his full name, he would reply, 'It's Michael actually'. Michael was meticulous and loved the fine detail of things.

Many years earlier the poor man had been on a night stop and was fast asleep when his hotel had caught fire. Everyone made it out alive but there had been issues with the emergency escape routes. It had understandably terrified him and, from that point on, he always carried an extra night-stop rucksack. It contained an abseiling rig with enough rope to enable him to escape from any third floor bedroom window. His equipment was added to over the

80

years as, for noise deadening reasons, hotels adopted sealed double-glazed units with no opening windows. To overcome this, his equipment now contained a natty little hammer device that could shatter the tempered glazing units. Presumably if required, he would don the abseiling gear, use the hammer thing and then fling himself out of the shattered window.

For this cunning plan to work, of course, it meant he was restricted to a bedroom no higher than the third floor and this would result in some very interesting conversations with the receptionist at check-in. Especially in countries whose national character traits were somewhat inflexible. Our industrial agreements with most hotels were for the pilots to be accommodated on the higher floors to get away from traffic noise. This agreement obviously came into direct conflict with Michael's personal need for a lower floor. Arguments would ensue with the receptionist saying 'rule are the rules', and him saying that he might be a crusty old captain but he didn't want to become a crispy old captain. He thought this phrase hilarious but of course it meant nothing to the receptionist who was unaware of his particular foible. He usually got his way when he asked them to find him another hotel.

On night stops with him, having survived the fiery inferno that didn't happen the previous evening, the crew would meet the following morning for pick-up, but Michael was never there. He would get up thirty minutes earlier than necessary and set off to walk to the airport. His reasoning was it was far more efficient to exercise this way.

It was up to us to try to spot him en-route so we could pick him up when we caught up with him. He was easy to spot as he was usually the only immaculately turned-out airline pilot walking along the dusty road with his ramrod straight back, captain's hat placed just so, freshly pressed trousers, and mirror shined shoes fending off the local dog nipping at his heals.

Anyway, back to the day of the route check, with me as captain. It didn't go smoothly at all. Nothing to do with our performance but because of the weather. Extreme winds across most of Europe made for a very challenging and uncomfortable day. Our approach into Bilbao was difficult. The turbulent high winds rolling off the adjacent hills meant we just couldn't keep the aircraft within normal limits. It was like riding a bucking bronco. We were being thrown about, straining against our five-point seat harnesses, aircraft jolting, wings rolling and dropping, me correcting, engines screaming to maintain our speed. With conditions getting worse nearer the ground, we called it and executed a go around, applied full power and climbed the aircraft safely away from the ground.

The second approach was pretty much identical to the first, and our passengers were understandably showing signs of stress.

Safely at altitude again, we took stock. We had enough fuel for a third approach before having to make for our diversion airfield but the question was, should we? The accepted protocol, (and our manuals hint this very strongly) is that if a landing is not going to be successful after the third attempt, a diversion should be carried out. The logic being that after three goes the outcome is very unlikely to be any different, and even the most seasoned and relaxed passengers will be fast approaching the end of their tether. As if reading our minds, the air traffic controller informed us that there had been a drop in wind speed and its direction was more in line with the runway. We made the third approach resulting in a successful, if not the smoothest, landing.

In order to make up for lost time we choked down our crew meal and started preparing for our return to London. All new flights start with a walk around the outside of the aircraft. We check for obvious abnormalities like fuel or hydraulic leaks, and that all removable panels are securely closed. We also check the general condition of the flight control surfaces and landing gear.

In all the excitement of the previous flight I had almost forgotten the lurking presence of Michael, our examiner, and his notebook that had a novel's worth of new entries. I tried to ignore the possible implications of his notes, telling myself he was a stickler for the minutiae and that whatever we had done wrong was in the past and we had to move on.

It was still blowing a gale outside and I had to lean into the wind, my trousers flapping madly like sails that had detached from their rigging, and my 'hi-vis' vest inflating like a parachute. I wasn't surprised that Michael joined me to observe the 'walk around'. He'd want to make sure I'd checked details like the tyres for correct tread depth.

And then suddenly, he was gone. I looked around and realised he had climbed up into the landing gear bay and was staring intently at some panel that I knew for certain didn't need to be stared at. After he had jumped down, he explained why, but as it was something that even the engineers would not consider necessary, even in their oily overalls, I didn't give it much attention. Just another of his quirky traits.

The flight back went without incident but by the time we found ourselves sitting in the debriefing room at Heathrow, we were really tired. Hoping against hope we wouldn't be there long, we were surprised when most of Michael's comments were positive and succinct. And then he had to spoil it:

'As you know, Nigel, uniform standards dictate that your hat should be worn at all times when outside and I noticed you didn't wear yours during the walk around in Bilbao.'

For the briefest of moments I thought he was kidding, but this was Michael, so I stopped myself laughing just in time.

'I absolutely agree Michael but on this occasion it was gusting up to 40 knots and I thought my hat would blow off and end up in another aircraft's engine.'

There was no lengthy argument, he simply stood up and walked out of the room. I wondered if I had offended him, or if he was going to return with the fleet manager. Surely he couldn't fail me for not wearing my hat? He soon returned to the room, not with the fleet manager but with two office fans, which he proceeded to set up on the table in front of me. He asked me to put on my hat, after which he turned on the fans. He pushed them closer and closer to my face until I started to feel like James Bond in 'Dr No' as the laser beam moves closer and closer to his privates.

It seemed this was proof that, as my hat didn't blow off, I could have, and should have, worn my hat during the walk around in Bilbao. I was so utterly bewildered I didn't know what to say. Apparently, I wasn't required to say anything. He simply got up again, told us we had passed, put on his hat and walked out of the room, leaving the fans running.

Shocked

We were in Prague and if you've been there, you'll probably agree it's a beautiful city. It was a pleasant summer's evening and the first officer, myself and a couple of male cabin crew had decided to have a beer in the old town square.

By this time, Prague had become a popular destination for UK stag weekends. So, I suppose it wasn't surprising that as a group of four men, we might be mistaken for lads about town. I say *might*, because I was in my early forties, dressed in a polo shirt, chinos and boat shoes. I couldn't have projected a more typical image of a middle class, middle-aged Englishman if I had tried. So, it came as a great surprise when a very young girl approached me.

'Do you want to do it?' she asked.

'Do what?'

She rolled her eyes like the young do.

'Do you want to have sex,' she said in that deliberate way we use when talking to the hard of hearing.

'NO,' I said in capitals to make my point.

'How about a blow job then?'

'NO. Go away.'

'What's the matter with you? Are you a weirdo?' she demanded before storming off.

I'm not sure what disturbed me the most. The fact that such a young girl should be driven to such lengths, or that my refusal was so unusual she had resorted to sarcasm.

FOD for Thought

A three-letter acronym is an abbreviation consisting of three letters, usually the initial letters, of the phrase being abbreviated. It amuses me that 'three-letter acronym' is abbreviated to TLA which is, of course, a TLA itself. LOL.

FOD is one of many three-letter acronyms used in the aviation world. It stands for Foreign Object Debris and can cause Foreign Object Damage. It's basically any loose object on a parking area, taxiway or runway that shouldn't be there. Foreign Object Debris can puncture tyres, jam moving parts or be ingested by aircraft engines with sometimes catastrophic results. One of the most infamous and tragic cases of damage to an aircraft from a foreign object was the loss of an Air France Concorde in 2000.

On its take-off roll, a strip of metal on the runway, which had fallen off the preceding aircraft, punctured one of the Concorde's tyres. The shockwave from the tyre blowout damaged electrical wiring, and one of its fuel tanks. The escaping fuel ignited, resulting in an uncontrollable fire. Very soon afterwards, damage was sustained to some of its flight control surfaces, and both left engines lost power. The aircraft crashed two minutes after take-off resulting in the loss of all 109 lives on board and a further four on the ground.

So, you can understand why FOD is taken very seriously. Even a plastic bag, or the smallest washer or cable tie can threaten aircraft safety, and none of it is tolerated. Before an aircraft arrives or leaves its parking stand, the area is meticulously checked for debris. There are now automated FOD detection systems that scan the runway for foreign objects, and at major airports a visual inspection is also performed several times a day.

At the London airports these visual inspections are carried out by specialist teams in bright yellow Range Rovers. They operate under the radio call sign of 'checker' and travel the length of the runway in stages, in between take-offs and landings. Often an aircraft is held at the end of the runway ready for take-off and told to wait while the 'checker' barrels towards them from the opposite end. It would take too long for them to travel the two mile length of the runway in one go, so they are ordered to 'vacate' to allow the waiting aircraft to get underway. At this point, the 'checker' turns 90 degrees off the runway and onto the grass with all the gusto of a world-class rally driver. They loiter at a safe distance until the aircraft screams past. Once clear, they race back onto the runway to continue their scan.

FOD can come in all shapes and sizes. Arriving into Heathrow after a lengthy holding delay one winter's evening, landing lights stabbing through the drizzle and misty gloom, we picked up movement on the right-hand side of the runway. We were on final approach at about 300 feet and 20 seconds to touchdown. Like some surreal theatre show, two foxes ran onto our 'stage', picked out in our spotlights. About half way across the runway, they became aware of our imminent arrival. It was probably my imagination, but I could swear I saw their eyes widen. They started to cartwheel their legs in a cartoon-style backward step, and then they turned tail and ran for it.

I knew it was going to be a close-run thing but decided on balance to continue with the landing, rather than execute a go around with minimal fuel reserves. We heard and felt nothing on touchdown but we reported it anyway. If you're going to strike anything it's normally a bird, so when I reported that I might have just landed on a fox, ATC were not sure they had heard me correctly and I had to repeat it several times.

FOD is FOD and so they immediately closed the runway, and ordered all the aircraft in trail behind us to execute a sequenced go around whilst they investigated. I'm sorry to report that we did in fact hit one of the foxes and it was found dead on the runway.

If I wasn't feeling wretched enough about it, word obviously got out because for the next few weeks I was addressed as Fox Killer by the cabin crew.

All Puffed Up

Being away from home for countless New Year's Eve celebrations did have one small compensation. Flying over Europe as midnight struck, the flight deck provided a bird's eye view of thousands of fireworks lighting up the sky to the far horizon.

It was a full flight back from Munich one New Year's Day, and we had just reached our cruise altitude of 38,000 feet. A crew member came in to tell us we had a bagpipe player on board. Apparently, he had been flown out to Germany especially to pipe in the New year, and he was now returning to the UK.

He kindly agreed to my request to play us all a tune. I made a PA to the passengers letting them know what was about to happen, and hoped they would enjoy the entertainment. I opened the flight deck door (which was allowed back then) to give half an ear to the performance. I knew we were in for a treat. He was travelling in full regalia and looked splendid. Standing in the aisle, he settled the pipes on his shoulder and began to inflate the bag. He huffed and puffed. And then he puffed and huffed some more, until he was red in the face and the veins in his neck were fit to burst, but he couldn't get the pipes to work. Not a note. After trying for several minutes, he shook his head in dejected defeat.

If I had known it was going to be a disaster, of course I would never have suggested it. It was only as the piper slunk back to his seat that I realised he had perfectly demonstrated the effects of low air pressure and density at cruise altitudes.

At a standard cruise altitude of say 35,000 feet the cabin is kept at a pressure equivalent to 8,000 feet. Most people see it as a bag of crisps straining at the seams, bloated by low air pressure.

On this occasion, we had inadvertently humiliated a Scotsman.

The whole sorry affair got me thinking. If 'The Three Little Pigs' had been set in the high Alps, it would have been a pretty rubbish fairy tale: 'The first little piggy couldn't be arsed to build a strong house because he knew if the wolf tried anything silly, he could huff and puff all he wanted, but he would only end up coughing up blood and collapsing from a near fatal aneurysm.'

Is it a Test?

'It's only like taking your driving test,' said the lady in training admin after I complained about the extremely short notice I had been given for my six-monthly simulator test.

I wondered which mini sub-state of the UK she lived in, where failing a driving test would mean being immediately stripped of your operating licence, the possible end of your career, and losing the means of supporting your family. Maybe the Isle of Man is that harsh, but I bet it isn't.

Failing a simulator exam is brutal. The first officer and I were sitting in the debriefing room, and I was trying to gauge the expression on the examiner's face. I was particularly knackered after working really hard guiding and cajoling the first officer through the last four hours of purgatory. We were there to renew our individual flying licences but we operated as a crew. Normally.

On this occasion, the first officer had seemed detached, and instead of being ahead of events, he was constantly behind. It was worse than working on my own because I was having to correct his mistakes. The examiner got the easy bit out of the way first: I had passed.

He then turned to my colleague and said, 'First Officer Smith, you have failed to reach the required standard for this revalidation and from immediate effect your licence to operate is withdrawn.'

That was it. One sentence.

Done.*

I later discovered this was the culmination of a pretty harsh week for him. He had just found out that his wife was having an affair with his best friend and, understandably, this was uppermost on his mind.

For him, 'failing his sim' was a devastating blow. On the other hand, it does mean that commercial aircraft are only operated by pilots who have demonstrated, on a painfully regular basis, the most stringent professional standards. Two days in the simulator every six months, testing our skill in every conceivable emergency scenario, including engine fires, and failures relating to every system on the aircraft, from electrical, hydraulic, flight control and flight computers, to landing gear, pressurisation, fuel leaks, and on and on.

We are tested on emergency manoeuvres to prevent head on collisions with other aircraft, and escape manoeuvres to avoid terrain and severe weather; how to cope with smoke and fire in the aircraft; how to deal with a bomb threat or hijacking, or volcanic ash, fog, snow, ice and wind. We also have to prove we can still fly, make an approach and land having lost the bulk of our primary instruments.

On top of this we are assessed on our team skills. Initially developed by NASA, these 'ideal behaviours' include leadership and teamwork, communications, problem solving, decision making and professional standards.

All this takes place in the simulator building at Heathrow. We recently moved to a spanking old building.

Old because it is grade two listed, and happened to be empty. It was repurposed and now looks like the closing sequence of the Indiana Jones movie *Raiders of the Lost Ark*, except instead of crates disappearing into the distance, there is a very long row of *War of the Worlds* triffid-like machines. They randomly rock and tilt on their hydraulic jacks, their calm and majestic manner at odds with the stress and concentration being generated inside them. I always think the place smells of fear.

Simulator testing aside, every year we have a training day to test our knowledge of the safety equipment on board, including our ability to tackle an oven fire, which always has special meaning for me.

And every year we must complete a lengthy technical knowledge module; pass a stringent medical and have a check ride with an examiner who sits in on a normal commercial flight.

Eight examined events a year, every year, and failing any one of them results in the loss of your flying licence.

But it's only like taking a driving test, apparently.

*After some personal time, the first officer was given a period of re-training. He went on to successfully complete the simulator tests and his licence was reinstated.

It's The Law

Taxiing out to the runway in Lisbon I got a call from a cabin crew member at the back of the aircraft. He was concerned about the behaviour of a group of twelve young men who were being very disruptive. He suspected some of them were drunk, their behaviour was borderline unacceptable and they were unsettling the other passengers. When he asked them to quiet down a little, they became abusive towards him. They did eventually calm down but he remained concerned because he had overheard one of them saying they would wait until they were in the air and then 'really kick off'.

Safety trumps everything in the airline business and I felt it was better to tackle any issues on the ground rather than face potential issues in the air. I obtained permission from air traffic control to pull off the main taxiway and park. I then handed over control to the first officer, donned my jacket and cap in order to look as official as possible and went into the cabin to assess the situation.

The legal powers bestowed on the aircraft commander (captain) are wide-ranging and far-reaching. In fact, the law states that from the time the aircraft doors are closed for departure until they are opened on arrival, anyone failing to obey a lawful command from the aircraft commander is committing a *criminal* offence under European and UK law.

The Civil Aviation Act makes any British registered aircraft in flight subject to United Kingdom criminal law. In addition, the Air Navigation Order states that criminal offences include being drunk on an aircraft; smoking when the 'No Smoking' sign is on, and behaving in a threatening, abusive, insulting or disorderly way towards the crew or other passengers. It may also surprise you to know that when the fasten seatbelt signs are illuminated, as far as the law is concerned, it is a direct command from the commander of the aircraft. Not returning to your seat and fastening your seatbelt is a criminal offence.

It was fairly easy to spot the young men - a group in their late twenties, all the size of rugby players. They were all wearing a 'uniform' of Oxford pattern shirts and either corduroy or chino trousers, and brown brogues. A few of them were garnished with chins, teeth and floppy hair that brilliantly complimented the social stereotype.

As I approached, I noticed some of them started to look distinctly uncomfortable and sheepish.

'Gentlemen,' I began. 'One of my crew is concerned about your behaviour. I have to decide whether to take you to London or off-load you here. I need you to assure me you are going to behave yourselves.'

A self-appointed spokesman who was the biggest of the lot, and obviously in control, replied: 'Ya, deffo, London, absolutely, isn't that right, Tarquin?'

The guy next to him nodded. He couldn't actually say anything because he had turned away and was puking into his sick bag. I've never seen anyone vomit so quietly or with such restraint in the confines of a small, economy seat.

'It's also an offence to be drunk on board an aircraft,' I added, looking pointedly at Tarquin.

Head boy replied, 'He's not drunk. Tarkers had one too many age-ed 'escargot.' He'll be OK. I promise you'll have no issue with us, El Capitaine.'

They were all looking like scolded children now.

'You should know that if there is any misbehaviour during the flight, I may divert the aeroplane and have you arrested. You will be committing a criminal offence which could carry a custodial sentence. Do you understand the gravity of the situation?'

Again, Spokesperson said, 'Absolutely Captain, you'll have no trouble from any of them, I promise. We are all acutely aware of what's at stake here.'

I looked at him quizzically but decided not to follow up on his remarks. Most of them nodded. Two of them heaved.

I later discovered the young men were city lawyers on a stag weekend, and they had obviously had a riotous time of it. They immediately apologised to the crew member for threatening to 'kick-off'. The possibility of facing criminal proceedings, with catastrophic consequences for their legal careers, no doubt rapidly sobered them up.

Four Hundred Words for Snow

It's said that the Inuit have fifty different words for snow. Apparently, the Scottish have more than four hundred words and expressions for snow – this is according to a project which is aiming to compile a Scots thesaurus. What a fantastically rich language it must be. I'm guessing the entry under 'sunshine' is ominously lacking, but when they get around to the deep-fried confectionary section, they are going to have a field day.

In many Scandinavian countries in winter, it often snows so much that it's hard to keep the runways clear. It's not unusual to have to use a runway that is covered in snow and while it isn't an exact science, the properties of various types of snow and ice have been measured, allowing calculations to determine whether it is safe to use. Airports can either measure how slippery the runway surface is by using specialised equipment, or a generic assumption can be made by assessing the different types and depth of snow and ice, be it dry snow, wet snow, slush or ice. From this, a 'coefficient of friction' (a measure of how slippery the runway surface is) can be obtained. Using this, along with ambient conditions and aircraft take-off weight, the required take-off distance can be calculated.

Just as crucially, if the take-off has to be abandoned for technical reasons just before lift-off, the distance required to stop the aircraft on a runway more akin to a skating rink can also be calculated. As you can imagine, this can be significant on icy runways. When added together, the combined distance to accelerate to take-off speed and then decelerate to a stop has obviously got to be less than the actual length of the runway. The technical term is ASDA, which has nothing to do with where you buy your cheesy wotsits. It is an acronym for Accelerate Stop Distance

Available - that is, the length of hard surface available to accelerate down the runway and then decelerate to a full stop.

So, 'on the day', take-off and stopping distances for an aircraft are always a variable feast that change with runway conditions, aircraft weight, air temperature and pressure. On the flight deck there is no accurate means of knowing how these distances equate to points on a particular runway and so an equivalent measure of speed is used. We know how quickly the aircraft can accelerate. If the take-off is going to be abandoned safely, the speed at which a decision must be made by is known as the V1 speed. Beyond that speed it is highly likely that the aircraft will run out runway before it comes to a stop.

As soon as the aircraft starts to move down the runway for take-off, it would be reasonable, when sat in the passenger cabin, to suppose 'this is it, we are on our way'. For us on the flight deck, this couldn't be further from our minds. In this safety critical environment, right up to the point where the aircraft can no longer be safely stopped on the runway (V1), all our thoughts and actions are focused on stopping the aircraft should events warrant it. We are all coiled springs ready to leap into action.

The non-handling pilot is focused on the instruments, looking for anything untoward, and especially for any sign of engine trouble. The pilot at the controls has his hand on the thrust leavers ready to slam them closed and ensure the automatic emergency breaking systems activate. If a decision to stop is made, he closes the thrust leavers, and then the non-handling pilot engages the reverse thrust, helping to slow the aircraft down. Spoilers are big plate sections on the top surface of a wing that can be extended upward into the airflow to disrupt the streamline flow and increase drag. On stopping, these should automatically deploy but if they don't, it's the non-handling pilot's job to deploy them manually.

There are only a handful of serious failures that would result in a high speed rejected take-off, for example an engine failure before V1, and for these, any flight crew member is authorised to command a rejected take-off by shouting 'STOP'.

With other, less severe failures, only the captain has the authority to decide whether the situation would warrant a stop or continue. In many cases, especially at high speed, it would be safer to continue with the take-off.

On pretty much all snow and ice contaminated runways, the speed at which the aircraft can be rotated to become airborne (VR) is significantly higher than the V1 speed.*

In other words, there is a critical time during the take-off where the aircraft is travelling too quickly to stop safely, but hasn't yet achieved the required speed to get airborne. And it is in that zone that we found ourselves one grotty day in Scandinavia. The left engine failed on us.

I've always thought the human brain is both incredibly complex but also extremely flawed when faced with some modern-day situations. Given a sudden stimulus, our brains have two routes to interpret that stimulus. The first one is primeval, hardwired, fast to react, and does so without our permission. I guess it's what's kept us alive over the millennia. It has encouraged us to run away from the big woolly mammoth instead of being flattened whilst debating whether to prod it with a piece of flint on a stick. In the modern-day environment however, these black-and-white, knee jerk actions are often not only of little use to us, they can also be downright dangerous.

It is the slower rational, analytical part of our brain that will come up with a workable solution to the complex problems of modern living. This is when the rule of initially doing nothing comes into its own. Whilst the primaeval part of the brain is screaming at us to do something, anything, it doesn't care what, if we resist it and do nothing, just for a split second, we give ourselves time for the analytical side of the brain to catch up. We give ourselves time to gather information, process, analyse and create a solution rather than rampaging off in an inappropriate direction. It's incredibly difficult to achieve because the primeval side of the brain is so powerful.

That's why we pilots train, and train, and train, and are then examined on the correct procedures and reactions to every phase of a flight. Before every single take-off, all commercial pilots rehearse and agree the procedures to be followed should a failure occur on the take-off run. It reinforces what we, as a team, will do together. This rehearsal pre-programmes the correct reactions to a situation where the primeval part of the brain would be screaming to do something ill-advised. And it is precisely why when we had an engine failure at the worst possible point on a snow-covered runway, our training kicked in. Even before the failure I was working hard. As we picked up speed along the runway, a blustery wind continually pushed the aircraft off the centreline and I had to make a conscious effort to be extra gentle on the rudder to correct for these deviations on the contaminated runway. I heard the first officer, Tom, call 'V1'. We were now beyond the stop point. I removed my hand from the thrust leavers and simultaneously he relaxed his left hand which was poised to engage reverse thrust should it be required. This is standard procedure to acknowledge we were no longer in a position to stop.

Suddenly I felt the aircraft lurch to the left. I heard the 'master warning' chimes indicating the warning system had something to tell us, and was aware of a red (most critical) message on the warning display. Tom shouted, 'engine failure'. Whilst all this was happening, I instinctively used rudder to correct the aircraft's swing, this time caused, not by the wind, but by the sudden loss of power from the engine.

We had to dig in, be disciplined and refuse to allow the primeval brain to take over. It was screaming at me to stop the airplane and be safe on the ground.

But I didn't slam the thrust leavers closed; we were beyond that point.

We didn't try to find out what had gone wrong; there would be time for that later.

We didn't try to determine which of the engines had failed; there would be time for diagnosis later.

No radio calls.

No chatter between ourselves.

No panic.

We waited for the speed to build.

We both knew the drill. We knew we could rely on each other to do the right thing, at the right time, in the right order.

I was looking outside in order to keep the aircraft straight on this skating rink of a runway. I also allowed myself the briefest scan of the instrument panel, my inner dialogue telling me:

'Some sort of engine issue.'

'The speed is definitely increasing.'

'Get your eyes back outside. Keep the aircraft straight.'

It felt like an age but finally Tom called 'rotate'. We had reached the required speed for flight.

Gently easing the aircraft into the air, at a much slower rate than usual due to the reduced power available, the aircraft became airborne.

Within seconds we were into cloud.

Blind to the outside world, I switched my eyes into the flight deck. We were now totally reliant on our instruments.

It's bread and butter stuff for a pilot to fly on instruments, but even for an experienced pilot, it takes a huge proportion of the brain's resources to process and build up a three-dimensional picture of the outside world from flight instruments alone. There are no traditional cues to gain a sense of up and down, left and right, fast or slow. Even the weight of your body can't indicate which way is up. Even when upside down, 'g forces' can pull you into your seat giving exactly the same feeling. Without any visual cues from outside, it's very easy for the body's balance system to become confused and tell lies.

I knew Tom was concentrating like a hawk, not only on me to make sure I was coping, but also on the instruments, waiting for the tell-tale readings from the altimeter and vertical speed indicator to say we were indeed airborne and climbing away. He confirmed this by simply saying, 'positive rate' [of climb].

Having achieved safe flight, the next crucial event was to retract the undercarriage. I ordered 'gear up', and having repeated the command back to me, Tom moved the gear lever to rid us of this huge source of drag that was now working against the thrust of the remaining engine.

Dig in. Check we were still at the correct climb speed; adjust if necessary; keep the wings level; check we were actually still climbing.

We were waiting for the magic two hundred feet; the certified safe height to engage the autopilot. Allowing the autopilot to fly the aircraft would release vital mental capacity to start the process of analysing what had just happened. Every six months in the simulator we are required to demonstrate we can do all this without the autopilot but it sure helps when it's available.

Our analysis of what had occurred started at the normal recommended minimum of four hundred feet, climbing safely away. It was vital to get an initial diagnosis of all the issues in order to secure and isolate any problems. As always, we did this as a team. Whilst I flew the aircraft through the autopilot, Tom pointed out all the relevant systems and indications.

An engine can fail in four different ways. Determining the failure affects how it is treated and which checklist to action. First and foremost, the correct failed engine had to be identified - absolutely critical on a two-engine aircraft, where shutting down the wrong, working, engine would have clearly catastrophic results. You might think this is obvious, but with the primeval brain still urging us to do something, anything, it doesn't care what, it would be very easy to make a rash choice if we were not absolutely disciplined.

We agreed that the engine hadn't simple 'wound down', nor was it on fire, yet. We could see from the engine instruments that a part of the rotating compressor section had stopped moving and its internal temperature was rapidly rising to 900°C, indicating a severe mechanical failure. A timely but measured response was going to be required if the failed engine was going to be made safe before it caught fire.

We agreed the diagnosis and I called for the relevant checklist. Tom started to work through it and as per our training, we cross-checked vital switches before Tom moved them. By shutting down the left engine we had isolated it and made it safe but at the same time, we had lost the electrical, hydraulic and pneumatic supplies it was producing. We started the small auxiliary engine so that it, and the remaining engine, could share the load. On passing

1,000 feet, I accelerated the aircraft to bring in the flaps, again another source of drag. After finishing the emergency and normal checklists, we contacted air traffic control to establish a safe holding pattern whilst we made a plan. Up to this point, no contact with air traffic control was either needed or wanted.

We use a fantastic acronym, TDODAR, to help us in all critical decision-making processes. It's worth mentioning because it can be used effectively for any day-today decisions. Granted it may be a slight overkill when choosing whether to have marmalade on your toast, but for complex situations, it's great. For us it went something like this:

T. Time. How much time did we have available to us? Did we need to make more time?

We had just started the flight and we didn't have a fuel leak so we had lots of fuel, we weren't on fire and although we had had an engine failure we were flying quite safely and therefore in no immediate danger. Time was of the essence, but not critical.

D. Diagnosis. What could we see, hear, feel, smell? What else could it be?

Very rarely an engine can simply run down, giving the possibility of restarting it but today we had already diagnosed a severe mechanical engine failure, and internal damage. There were no other diagnostic alerts that would indicate any secondary failures such as damage to the flight control surfaces.

O. Options. Look at all the possible options. What are the risks? Will any of these not work and why?

At this point in the process, all the various options were generated and discussed. It's vital that all pilots on the flight deck take part in this free flow of ideas and come up with as many options as possible. One option is always to do nothing, but in our case the regulations were very specific: On a two-engine aircraft, the failure of one engine necessitates the landing at the nearest suitable airport.

There are several factors in determining whether an airport is 'suitable'. As pilots we are trained to always project ahead and during our preflight tasks we had already calculated that even with the current snowy conditions the runway was long enough to land on, and the weather conditions, albeit poor, were good enough for us to make an approach and landing.

Our regulations state that to land on a runway designated as slippery, both reverse thrusts need to be operational. With one reverse thrust unavailable because of the shut-down engine, this might have been an issue. Luckily, although the runway was covered in snow and breaking efficiency would be reduced, it was not designated 'slippery'.

D. Decide. Decide which of the options is the best one, and state it clearly.

Again, in our case we had already worked out that despite the runway being full of ice and snow, our weight, runway conditions and weather were such that we could land safely using one engine.

A. Assign tasks. And be aware of assigning too much and creating work overload.

I asked Tom to prepare the aircraft for its approach and landing, I briefed air-traffic control on our intentions, and also briefed the cabin crew to prepare the aircraft for the landing. Finally, I explained to our passengers what had happened, what we were about to do, and what was required of them.

R. Review. This is one of the most important parts of the decision-making process. It allows for a regular recap: were our goals going to be achieved with our current plan or did they need modifying?

It was during this discussion that we decided not to use full reverse thrust on the working engine after landing as it might cause steering difficulties on the snow-covered runway.

I'm pleased to say that the approach and landing went as per our plan, and we arrived back on stand within an hour of leaving it.

I've included this story to hopefully reassure any nervous flyers out there that whilst it was a dramatic event, it is something that we train for regularly in the simulator. Consequently, there was a defined and ordered way of operating that resulted in a safe and controlled solution.

*There are three critical speeds used at take-off. They are calculated using air temperature, airfield elevation, aircraft weight and runway conditions.

V1 is the decision speed beyond which stopping is no longer possible and the aeroplane is committed to fly. So whatever happens after V1, even a failure of an engine, you dig in, continue the take-off and sort out any issue in the air.

VR is the speed is at which the nose of the aircraft is raised and the aeroplane is rotated into a climb attitude.

V2 is the speed that will be flown if an engine failure occurs. It guarantees a safe flying speed along with a (sometimes small) rate of climb.

The Northern Lights

I wonder how many bucket lists include a wish to see the Northern Lights? From the flightdeck we were incredibly fortunate to have a bird's eye view of these otherworldly 'curtains' of swirling, rippling lights. They were constantly shape-shifting, sometimes falling like sheets of vivid green rain, at other times snaking across the sky like the giant serpent that encircled the world in Norse mythology. The northern lights, or Aurora, have inspired countless stories and folklore down the centuries.

The Inuit believe the souls of the dead dance in the Aurora, which they call 'aksarnirq'. Sometimes the spirits are carrying torches to guide those still in this world. At other times, they are playing football with a walrus skull as they dance across the sky. 'Aksarnirq' translates as ball player.

In Finland the word for the Aurora is 'revontulet' which means 'fox fire'. Legend has it that as the fire fox's tail touches the ground, it sparks and glows, and as he leaps into the night the fire spreads across the sky.

And the indigenous peoples of Canada and the US believe the Aurora is telling them they are not alone; that there is something beyond this earthly realm waiting for them after death. A rather lovely, comforting sentiment.

It wasn't until the beginning of the twentieth century that a Norwegian called Kristian Birkeland proposed a scientific explanation for the Aurora Borealis as they are known in the northern hemisphere, and Aurora Australis in the southern hemisphere.

He quite rightly deduced that the northern lights are caused by activity on the surface of the sun. Particles flowing from the sun get caught up in the Earth's magnetic field, and are swept towards the north and south poles. The aurora's characteristic wavy patterns and 'curtains' of light are caused by the lines of force in the magnetic field.

The northern lights can be multicoloured but are predominantly green because as the electromagnetic radiation from the sun hits the atoms in the air each individual atom is temporarily excited into a higher energy form. That energy is then released in the form of light. Nitrogen makes up eighty percent of the earth's atmosphere and it's the green wavelength of light that's emitted from the nitrogen atoms.

But, despite the scientific explanation, they always filled me with a sense of wonder and awe every time I was lucky enough to watch them from the flight deck.

Close Friends

I had just taken my seat as a passenger on a low-cost carrier flight. Other passengers started to settle into their own seats and I was now playing Russian Roulette – who was going to sit next to me? Would it be the man in the sleeveless tee-shirt, armpits slick with sweat, or the man with the streaming cold? Perhaps it would be the child who paved the way by flicking snot before him. Would it be Halitosis Man or The Farter? I had just begun to think I had got away with it, when the cabin went dark and a mountain of a man loomed over me. He was wearing a Popeye short sleeve shirt; his muscular legs clad in trousers so tight the seams were straining.

'My seat is next to yours,' he said in an Arnold Schwarzenegger accent.

'Ah,' I mouthed, and feigned surprised delight.

And so began three hours of an Englishman's social torture. The man's bulk demanded not only his seat but a large portion of mine too, and of course we were both wearing short sleeved shirts so our bare arms rubbed against each other. I squirmed, cowered and tried to shrink as much as I could but to no avail. Our arm hair was mingling. Sadly for me, he didn't appear to be concerned about personal space, or lack of it. He must have had a long day because he was a little ripe and, to cap it all, just after take-off, out came a picnic of rank salamis, pickles and fish-based sandwiches. Mmm, I thought, that's going to do wonders for his digestive system in about an hour's time.

It's Not All Sunshine and Roses

All in all, I would spend eight years on short-haul flying the Airbus. The first five years as a first officer, and the remainder as a captain. I felt ready to become a captain. I loved the extra responsibility and the richer dimension that came with the post.

Shortly after gaining my command, I managed to secure another 'promotion'. As a training captain, it was my responsibility to take candidates who had just passed the simulator course and train them to the required standard for their final route check. If they passed, they could then be released onto 'the line' for normal commercial flights.

I loved the training job. I prided myself on giving the trainees an empathic, structured environment in which to learn and thrive. It was very rewarding.

However, the post was fairly short lived, as after just two years the department was streamlined. It became more efficient and was now carrying too many training captains. I was in the right place for the 'last in first out' rule, and found myself back as a regular line pilot. I was finding the short-haul lifestyle increasingly relentless, and family life was suffering with Pen effectively a single parent for much of the time. It reached a point where I hadn't had a weekend off for more than eight months, which was ironic considering one of the reasons for transferring to short-haul was to have more time at home. Coupled with the sheer aggravation of fighting with other elements within the airline in order to get the job done, I was becoming increasingly restless once again.

The five-day tours involving eighteen flights were becoming a real issue. On one of those trips, the day having begun at four in the morning in a European city I cannot now recall, I found myself at Heathrow, re-grouping for the second of four flights that day. It was the norm not to stay with the same aircraft on arrival back at Heathrow. We had to transfer to the next aircraft by company bus, and the drivers worked to strict industrial rules. We would often see the driver sitting in the bus just meters away, reading a paper because they had completed the one, or however many onerous journeys, they were contracted to complete that hour.

Short-haul is very prone to delays either from ATC slots in Europe; holding delays at Heathrow; weather or a myriad of other things, and even the smallest delay on each sector compounded the situation as the day went on. And to be delayed still further because a bus driver was glued to his newspaper was infuriating. At their convenience, we would lug our bags off one aircraft, be rushed at twenty miles per hour to the next one, lug our bags up the aircraft steps, and go hell for leather to try to make up some time.

Other things were also beginning to niggle. Flight crew and cabin crew belonged to different and sometimes seemingly competing departmental empires and it meant that, for flying staff, there was never any unifying force. On top of that, we operated under wildly differing industrial agreements, meaning we were allocated work and carried out our daily rosters using totally different rules. On a single day we could work with three different groups of cabin crew. We were never able to build any meaningful team spirit, and often found ourselves in conflict in a silly power struggle of trivialities.

On one occasion, I was listening to the cabin address by one of the pursers. She knew I was listening and delighted in telling the passengers she was in charge of the aircraft today. Later I quietly mentioned to her, just to make sure we all fully understood the chain of command, that as captain, I was in charge of the aircraft. She said she'd meant she was in charge of the cabin. I politely reminded her that as the captain, I was in charge of the whole aircraft, not just the pointy bit at the front, and that she was carrying out her cabin duties on behalf of the captain.

It sounds petty and trivial but I knew from past experience that safety critical decisions had been made in the cabin without the knowledge of the flight crew, and those decisions could have had serious consequences. This just showed the level of the power games being played back then. A few weeks later, the first officer and I flew from

Paris to Heathrow. Our next sector was Düsseldorf but we didn't make it because of bad weather, and diverted to Cologne instead. From there we flew back to Heathrow and finally on to Milan for another night stop. For the final Heathrow to Milan sector - our fourth of the day - we picked up yet another cabin crew who were operating this, their one and only flight that day. Due to our earlier diversion, we were running late, and by the time we landed in Milan, our (the pilots) duty day was butting up against the maximum allowable. Even if we reduced our rest to the absolute minimum legally required, the following day's flight would have to be delayed.

We were awoken the next morning by a phone call from the airport duty manager who explained that due to the cabin crew industrial agreements, they had already been picked up from the hotel by taxi, and had flown home as passengers. We were going to be provided with a 'fresh' crew. Considering they had only operated a single sector in two days of work, I thought the original crew must have been pretty fresh, but to be fair to them, they were only doing what their agreements dictated. We carried on with our four sectors that day.

Recently I was reminded by a colleague, Al, (who is now a captain) that when he was fresh out of flying school, we flew together on one of his very first training flights. On the third sector up to Aberdeen I was hungry, and looking forward to savaging my crew meal. But it hadn't been loaded onto the aircraft, meaning we would have to wait until we landed. But on the ground in Aberdeen, I was informed by the station manager that she wasn't authorised to supply pilots' meals and we would have to organise something once we were back at Heathrow. By now I was very hungry, my blood sugars were extremely low, and I was starting to feel sluggish. I was in no mood to negotiate.

'No problem,' I replied calmly. 'Just put the delay down to catering please.' I stood up and put my jacket on.

'What delay, Captain?' she asked, looking worried.

'I'm sorry, but for safety reasons I really need to eat something and if there is no catering, we're going to go into the terminal and have some dinner. We'll be as quick as we can but I expect we'll be about thirty minutes.'

Five minutes after the manager had picked her jaw up from the floor, miraculously two meals arrived! Hey presto, we left on schedule and we got to eat, but it shouldn't have been such a battle.

Eureka!

I was finding short-haul increasingly hard work, relentless and utterly exhausting, and I was tired of constantly fighting battles just to get through the day. I think the Eureka moment finally came when, having been woken up at four in the morning in Amsterdam, I was now at Heathrow, preparing for the second flight of the day. And it was still only 8am. Feeling rather jaded, I watched one of our long-haul B777 pulling onto stand and I realised that although he had been flying through the night, we had both effectively missed a night's sleep. He was going to be heading home soon and I had three more sectors ahead of me.

Due to the cost (to the company) of putting me through the command course, I had been barred from moving fleets for three years, but that time was up. I now had the seniority, and had already talked to Pen about going back to long-haul. And so, looking at that big grown-up aircraft, and feeling how I did at that moment, I decided to make the change.

2003-2020
Boeing 777, Captain

The **Boeing 777** is the world's largest twin jet airliner, and was the first Boeing to be controlled by fly by wire. It holds the record for the longest (non-commercial) non-stop flight of any passenger airliner, flying 13,422 miles, the long way round from Hong Kong, over the Pacific, continental U.S., and the Atlantic to London. A flight lasting twenty-two hours and forty-two minutes. Our latest version, the 777-300ER has a maximum commercial range of 8,480 miles, can accommodate 396 passengers, and is powered by the world's most powerful jet engine. Each engine has the same diameter as the Boeing 737 cabin interior and can produce thrust equivalent to 110,000 horsepower. A typical family car produces 120 horsepower.

Our destinations are worldwide, from San Francisco in the west, Buenos Aires in the south, Sydney in the East, and all points in between. We also fly to Calgary and Montreal but neither of these is the most northerly airport on our long-haul routes. That accolade surprisingly goes to London Heathrow.

Cabin Fever

The conversion course for the B777 started with an intensive two-week self-teach technical course, followed by an exam. It basically involved sitting in a small windowless room with a cardboard mock-up of the flight deck and a touch screen monitor. The course was designed to be done in pairs, but the guy I was supposed to be partnering had withdrawn at the last minute. That meant me sitting on my own in a small cupboard for two weeks, which was fine to start with but rapidly became a little weird.

Automated video presentations were given on all the various technical aspects of the aircraft such as electrics, hydraulics, flight control and navigational systems and, being Boeing, the narrator was American. Along the way the programme checked my understanding by asking me to identify a switch, component or procedure on the touchscreen monitor. If I made the wrong selection the American voice would say 'touch the highlighted area', helpfully pointing out the correct response.

'Touch the highlighted area' became a regular theme as the days droned on, and it was hammered deeper and deeper into my psyche. Halfway through the course I began to suffer from cabin fever. I had nicknamed the narrator Todd and every morning, just as the door closed on the outside world for the day, I would sit at the monitor and say, 'Good morning, Todd, what exciting revelations have you got for me today?' Todd would blink his curser eagerly, beckoning me to 'press any key to continue'.

'Ah Todd, you are such a hoot.'

I would amuse myself by deliberately selecting the wrong answer and then shouting loudly in an American accent, 'Geez what an asshole, touch the highlighted area, dip shit'. On several occasions I was interrupted by a polite knock on the door and a voice asking if everything was OK.

'OK? Yes, everything is OK, why wouldn't it be OK? I haven't seen a human being all day but yes, everything is OK. Whoever you are, would you like to go for a coffee?'

Points Make Prizes

Todd has clearly done his job well, because I had passed the ground technical exam, completed the three-week simulator conversion course and the route flying section consisting of twelve commercial flights, and was now flying my final route check - a fully commercial flight with an examiner. If I passed, I would be let loose on my own £200 million aircraft.

I was rostered a New York JFK trip. On the outbound sector, I revelled in the technological advances since I had last crossed the Atlantic in the TriStar. The B777 was equipped with the latest GPS navigation systems along with satellite communication and automatic waypoint position reporting. It basically meant that once on the Atlantic track system, the aircraft would navigate itself extraordinarily accurately and relay our position without us having to lift a finger.

As with most large American airfields, there are always several possibilities for the approach and landing runway, and it often seemed to be a state secret which one would be allocated. Therefore, they all had to be planned for, pitfalls identified and briefed. It was then a case of waiting for ATC to allocate one, so the navigation and performance computers could be confirmed as correct, or reprogrammed. Not unusually, a few minutes later, ATC would change their minds and allocate a different runway, and the whole process had to be started all over again. Ultimate flexibility was required as there was always a high probability it would change yet again, and at the very last minute.

Being totally unfamiliar with JFK, and on an exam flight, it stood to reason that we were allocated the fairly infamous Canarsie approach. It's much more straightforward these days with the advent of GPS assisted curved approaches. Back then it was a half visual, half beacon assisted approach that curved around Jamaica Bay, ending with a fairly rapid transition from a banked turn to wings level just before landing. Large commercial passenger aircraft are not really designed for such breakneck manoeuvres so it's an unusual and exciting approach. Thankfully it all worked out.

As you know, my one and only time in Manhattan, fifteen years previously, had involved accompanying a bitter and twisted flight engineer hellbent on hiding his wealth from his soon to be ex-wife. With just twenty-four hours off on this visit, I was determined not to get waylaid again, and dashed around the city ticking off as many sites as I could, just in case it was another fifteen years before my next visit.

The last time I was there, my brief glimpses of Manhattan were of some dystopian, Gotham City inspired dump. It was filthy, the people slump shouldered and furtive, and it was said a walk around Central Park would end at the pearly gates. But now the city felt vibrant, the people energetic and friendly, the streets clean (well for a city anyway), and Central Park an absolute joy.

New York is everything you expect it to be, and it is one of my favourite cities in the world. If I had to sum it up in one sentence, I would say it's just like seeing it on TV. An odd statement I know, but the streets seem strangely familiar. Busy, hundreds of yellow cabs, traffic everywhere, people everywhere, hotdog stalls, steam rising from manholes, delicatessens, the distinctive accent, the sirens of the NYPD patrol cars. You can feel the power and vibrancy thrumming through the skyscrapers. Those skyscrapers, featured so often in films, appear before you at every turn. And if you are a 'Friends' fan, don't forget Pottery Barn, selling all those non-essential items from 'days of yore'.

Marvellous.

The flight back home was of no great consequence and all went well. Although I do remember taxiing out to the take-off position whilst being subjected to manic and over-excited ground controlling – something I would become familiar with over the coming years. The controllers at JFK assume you know the airfield inside out, and fire instructions at you like a Gatling gun. Instructions which often include safety critical information. Clearly, I was very new to the aircraft, very new to the airfield, and on my final route check. I was being quite cautious. When the ground controller started to rant at me for not making enough progress I apologised:

'I'm really sorry, it's my first visit here for fifteen years, and I'm not familiar with the airfield. If it's all the same to you, I would rather get things right slowly than get things wrong quickly.'

The examiner thought this hilarious because it was the only time in his experience that any ground controller at JFK was rendered speechless.

Back at Heathrow, on stand with the engines shut down, the examiner simply said, 'Well done Nigel, welcome to the 777 fleet'.

A great feeling.

It's All Relative

Buenos Aires is thirty-five degrees of latitude south of the equator. Flying back from there one night I noticed something odd about the star constellation Cassiopeia. Instead of it being the familiar 'W', it was in the shape of an M, and it was also back to front. Now I know there will be some pretty keen astronomer types out there saying, 'well der', but it took me a while to figure out what was going on.

And this is what I think was going on: If you were driving over the North Pole, the ground would be below you and the sky above - obviously. That would also hold true if you were driving over the South Pole. Wherever you are on Earth, gravity makes sure that earth is down and sky is up. But zoom out so you are looking at the globe of Earth from space, with the North Pole at the top.

Imagine the Earth is a beach ball. If you placed a model car on the ball's North Pole and then drove it around the ball to the South Pole, from your zoomed out view, the car is now upside down. Being in an actual car (or aircraft) the brain doesn't see this because it references everything from known information, and if your brain says you can't possibly be upside down, then the stars must be.

And why are the constellations back to front? Well, if you are at the North Pole looking south, then east is on your left. If you are on the South Pole looking north, then east is on you right. Again, your brain is saying the stars have flipped and not you. Enough already, go and have a cup of tea.

Take a Breather

We all know that at cruising altitudes, the environment outside the aircraft is hideously antisocial. It's -57°C, and there is so little oxygen that our time of useful consciousness could be as little as ten to fifteen seconds. And yet, as passengers, we sit there in our shirt sleeves watching a film and eating salted nuts, and we don't give it a second thought. And it's a testament to the technical marvel of the modern jet aircraft that we don't have to.

The only time we could conceivably be exposed to this harsh environment is if the aircraft suddenly lost pressurisation. It's a long shot because there are several backup systems to ensure it doesn't happen, but it's something pilots train for regularly in the simulator.

In an oxygen poor environment, time of useful consciousness is the time after which the brain can no longer make corrective and protective actions. Think back to the aircraft safety demonstration most people never watch because they are still fighting their neighbour for elbow real estate. It tells you that if the oxygen masks drop down you should put your own mask on first.

It is not because the airlines want you to be selfish and shout, 'Screw you, I'm alright Jack'. It is because if you don't get your mask on first, and sharpish, any inclination to help anyone else will be pointless because you will be unconscious in your seat. Mind you, if you are British, you are doomed because this is what will happen: The masks drop, two hands go up for the same mask, and collide.

A polite and stereo, 'Oh I'm sorry.'

Uncomfortable smiles. Then, 'After you.'

'No, after you, really.'

Then... blank.

Droning On

After a lifetime of flying, I still marvel at the brilliance of the modern aircraft. The engines are operating in the same inhospitable atmosphere and yet they suck in air at well over a tonne per second. Inside a typical commercial jet engine, at full chat, the combustion chamber burns fuel at up to six tonnes an hour and can create temperatures of around 2,000°C.

Pause for a moment to consider that the metal components of the chamber melt at around 1,300°C. So, what stops the whole thing from smearing itself past your porthole window like a melted candle? Magic, that's what. Well, and some advanced cooling techniques employed by some very clever engineers.

Aircraft engines are now so reliable that some years ago something happened that most people didn't even question. Long-haul aircraft used to be exclusively four engine beasts, like the Boeing 747 or Airbus A340. Now most long-haul aircraft only have two engines and are certified to operate up to one hundred and eighty minutes, that's three hours, from a diversion airport. They achieve this certification by having extra backup systems and maintaining an impressive reliability record. The airlines are happy because they are spending much less on fuel, and that makes the environment a little happier too.

Tactically however, things are a little more involved. With a four-engine aircraft, if one goes pop, there are three remaining. The crew, legally, have an option of carrying on to their destination. That would not be prudent with a two-engine aircraft and is quite rightly not allowed. The rules say if a two-engine aircraft has a failure of one of those engines, the aircraft should be landed at the nearest suitable airport - notwithstanding that the airport could technically be three hours away. In practical terms, most of the routes we fly would have a diversionary airport significantly closer. As the flight progresses, pilots continuously assess these airports for weather, runway conditions and facilities; those on top of the list a moment ago being discarded for more suitable ones. It's a constant game of hopscotch.

WhatsUp?

We were on our way to Shanghai, operating with the new contracted cabin crew who are generally, but not exclusively, a younger crowd. We buzzed one of the girls into the flight deck.

She said, 'I'm starting a WhatsApp group so we can organise a time to go out to dinner.'

'I don't have WhatsApp,' I replied.

'You er, what did you say?' She looked aghast, as if I'd just told her I didn't have a flying licence and was an impostor.

'I'm sorry, I don't have WhatsApp.'

'Oh... We're just trying to organise a time to meet up for dinner,' she persisted.

Perhaps she thought I hadn't understood her the first time. Or perhaps she was feeling sorry for me, convinced that without WhatsApp I would surely starve.

'What time were you thinking?' I asked.

'We thought about six o'clock.'

'Six o'clock it is then.'

'Oh... kay then.'

That evening, at five minutes to six, like the Red Arrows re-joining formation after their individual medley, we three pilots converged on the crew room to find two of the female crew members already there. Both were concentrating on their phones with an intensity bordering on fanatical. One was twirling her hair round her finger; the other was venting excess energy by pumping her left leg up and down at a rate that would have made a woodpecker jealous. She looked up briefly from her phone and, by way of greeting, said, 'Tamara and Karen are still doing their hair and will be another twenty-five minutes. Laura and Fi are still out shopping and won't be back for another twenty minutes. Tom is still in the gym and there are three more who want to come but are going to be late.'

I marvelled at her lung capacity because this was all relayed like a stream of consciousness, in one sentence and one breath.

'OK, well, we are hungry so we are going now and maybe see you all at the restaurant later?' I replied.

She looked up from her phone and said, 'Yeah, okay'.

And back to her phone. I've learnt over the years that this free flow approach to social arrangements is the norm and it doesn't bother me. Either they are there or they are not. The one constant is that the pilots will be there as agreed and that's good enough.

In The Dead of Night

I've always loved how much there is to see when flying at night. In the cruise part of a long night-flight, with the manic and high stress departure behind us, things would begin to calm down, and the relatively quiet cruise period would settle into an almost meditative sense of peace. The passengers had been fed and were now either watching a movie or trying to sleep. The cabin crew were on over-watch duties. The flight deck was dark, warm and quiet, the techno-glow of the instruments reassuringly saying 'all is good with the world'. Wrapped in this reassuring cocoon, the world treated me to some of its most breathtaking sights.

Sunsets were consistently mind blowing. When flying west at high latitudes, where degrees of longitude tick by at a rapid rate, we would literally chase the sun, and sunsets could last for hours. Eventually the sun would win out and it would slowly slip below the horizon, casting a shadow of the earth onto the atmosphere above. Sunset would transition to twilight, and in the aviation world of absolutes and labels we can't just have one twilight, we have three: civil, nautical and astronomical. Whilst it might detract from the pure cerebral joy of the earth resplendent in its afterglow finery, I think it's interesting that these definitions of twilight hark back to the days of sailing ships and sextant navigation.

Civil twilight (dusk) is the period when the sun's disc has just slipped below the horizon and its centre is six degrees below the horizon. There is enough residual sun light for terrestrial object to remain visible to the human eye without the need for artificial lights. Some of the brightest stars start to become visible.

During Nautical twilight (dusk) the centre of the sun's disc is between six and twelve degrees below the horizon, and is the last chance to make navigational reference to the horizon, as beyond this point it becomes indistinguishable. The human eye may be able to make out vague ground objects but any meaningful activity is not possible without artificial lighting. More stars are visible.

Astronomical twilight (dusk) occurs when the centre of the sun's disc is between twelve and eighteen degrees below the horizon. It is dark enough for all visible stars to be observed. Beyond that we have nightfall.

During dawn twilight and sunrise all the above remain true but in reverse order. These are all incredibly important markers for those reliant on navigating the oceans using those most basic of instruments.

The best time to see the Northern Lights is mainly in the winter months and, not to detract from their beauty and magnificence, they were a relatively common sight for us. A much rarer sight was a noctilucent sky. This is also a night time phenomenon, but they only appear in the summer months at mid to high latitudes. Noctilucent clouds, made up of tiny water ice crystals, populate the mesosphere (a height of some 260,000 feet) and are the highest occurring clouds in the atmosphere. During astronomical twilight it is possible for an observer to be in the earth's shadow and therefore in the dark, but for these high level clouds to be in sunlight. It's during this short twilight period that noctilucent clouds shine with an almost ethereal quality. Appearing silvery blue, I can only describe them as a dense spiders web run through with streaks and waves. I've only seen them twice, and they are rather special.

I have an app which shows star positions, satellite tracks and meteor fields, and what a thrill to have a front row seat to watch a meteor shower unfold. One evening the app told us that the International Space Station would pass by on a similar track to ours, so at the appointed time I looked to my left and saw it approaching at speed, high above us. It cruised past, and very quickly disappeared into the distance. If an aircraft is a technical marvel, what the space station?

There have been many manmade night sights, not all uplifting.

To see natural gas being burnt off in vast quantities in the major oil producing countries of the world is always a hugely depressing sight. It seems such a waste of a finite fuel source, it's highly polluting and it's needlessly contributing to global warming. We should be better than that. But to end on a high, I have flown over densely populated areas on July Fourth, New Year's Eve, Diwali,

Guy Fawkes and Chinese New Year. The line of sight at cruising altitude is around two hundred and forty miles in every direction and to see it erupt all at once with countless fireworks is truly remarkable. I remember one festival where a thin layer of low cloud masked the ground. From our lofty vantage point, we were among the fortunate few to watch hundreds of rockets burst through the clouds. Their vibrant colours reflected off them, illuminated the sky and gave us our own private display.

Thinking Outside the Box

At the crew briefing before the flight from Gatwick to Dallas, I mentioned that the UK clocks would go back from British Summer Time to GMT the evening we flew home, so instead of landing at seven o'clock UK time it would be six o'clock. One of the crew asked if that meant the flight would be an hour shorter. I initially assumed they were joking so I laughed in a 'ha-ha, good one' way, but when I glanced at their expression, I wasn't so sure.

Fast forward, and we were in the crew bus on the way to the hotel in Dallas. It had been a full flight and the cabin crew had worked hard. Two of the crew were saying they hadn't eaten very much on the flight and were looking forward to getting a McDonalds. This prompted another crew member, Jane, to join in with a story. She explained that on her last trip she and two colleagues had walked twenty-five minutes to the nearest McDonalds. When they arrived, they were dismayed to find it was a 'drive through only' restaurant and the staff wouldn't take their order at the serving hatch because they weren't in a car. Not to be defeated they walked around the corner to the intercom and tried to make an order whilst one of them made engine noises in the background. Not surprisingly this didn't work.

Next, using admirable problem-solving skills, they summoned an Uber and a few minutes later were chauffeured to the hatch to claim their prize of Mac and fries. They then climbed out of the Uber, paid the driver, and walked back to the hotel. Someone asked why they hadn't taken the Uber back to the hotel and saved themselves a twenty-five minute walk.

'Oh… yeh, we didn't think of that!'

Where Do You Think You're Going?

I had organised to take Penny away with me on a four-day trip to Chicago. It's a fantastic city at any time of the year, but the festivities of Thanksgiving weekend would make it even more special. We had arranged for Penny's parents to come down from Yorkshire to look after the kids.

Penny's story: As I boarded the plane, I overheard a conversation about another passenger: 'She has been deemed inadmissible by immigration so we are sending her straight back to the US on your flight.'

Now airborne, I was settled in my first-class seat enjoying a meal I hadn't cooked and a film that didn't involve Pokemon. My reverie was interrupted by a PA:

'If there is a medical doctor on board, could they make themselves known to the cabin crew?'

'That doesn't sound good,' I thought.

Just under two hours into the flight I looked at the onboard route map and realised we had made a 90 degree turn and were now pointing at Iceland.

'That's really odd,' I thought.

I went to the loo, and when I came out, there was Nigel talking to a young man in smart casual clothing.

Nigel asked him: 'So do you think you can fly the plane or not?'

OK, this was getting weird.

Nigel's story: I was told we had an 'inadmissible' passenger on board. A lady in her early thirties whose paperwork was not in order and so was not going to be allowed into the UK. We were to take her straight back to the USA.

We had entered the North Atlantic Track System, completed all the checks and radio calls and were settling down for a period of relative calm. Time for a nice cup of tea, I thought.

The intercom chimed. It was the cabin manager: 'A passenger has just reported that the inadmissible passenger has taken a large number of pills and downed half bottle of whisky. We have tried talking to her but she is not very responsive.'

'OK, see if you can find out what the pills were and make a PA asking if we have a doctor on board, and we'll start on a diversion plan,' I replied.

We knew that Keflavik, Iceland, was five hundred miles to the north. We had already made it our diversion choice for the time being, as it was the closest airport with good weather and a sufficiently long runway. As the passenger's condition sounded serious, we thought the chance of a diversion was high and so we contacted air traffic control to ask what they would let us do navigation-wise.

As I've mentioned previously, flying on these Atlantic flight tracks is beyond radar surveillance and strictly controlled. We were surprised therefore to be told there was no conflicting traffic to the north and should we wish to, we could cut straight across the other tracks direct to Keflavik. But this clearance would only be valid for the next twenty minutes.

Next, we discussed how we would program the navigation computers to get us to Keflavik. As the planned flight would be cut short, we would arrive at Keflavik with lots of unburnt fuel and would be too heavy to land. We discussed how much fuel to dump overboard in order to land at our maximum authorised landing weight. We could then calculate our landing speed and stopping distance.

The interphone chimed again: 'A doctor is with her now. We've found an empty bottle of sleeping pills. She is lapsing into unconsciousness and the doctor is advising we get her to a hospital as soon as possible,' the cabin manager explained.

A diversion it was to be, then. We quickly checked the weather was still OK at Keflavik, and air traffic control gave us a formal clearance to execute our agreed plan and head north. They said they would contact Keflavik about our intention to land with a medical emergency.

We now had a small window to start thinking ahead again. I worked out how long it would take to get to Keflavik, get the lady off the aircraft to hospital, refuel, replan and then carry on to Chicago. My calculations were met with an uncomfortable look from Tim the first officer.

It turned out that he was doing this trip on overtime. He had had the legal amount of rest required since his previous flight but not enough to allow me, the captain, to extend his duty hours much beyond those already planned. He wouldn't be able to go all the way to Chicago after Keflavik. I contacted company operations on the sat-phone, told them the story and asked them to look into getting us to somewhere on the east coast of America, say Boston or New York. At least we would be part the way there and could finish the journey after we had had some rest. The reply came back that as it was Thanksgiving all the American stations were reporting no spare accommodation for nearly three hundred passengers at such short notice.

OK, think further outside the box. I remembered that one of our passengers was a B777 first officer going on holiday. I contacted company operations who agreed that if he was rested and fit, he could act as a third pilot for the cruise portion of the flight from Keflavik to Chicago. That would allow us more duty hours - possibly enough to get all the way to Chicago.

I left the flying with Tim and went into the forward galley to ask if the first officer would be willing to help out. I guess I was naive to imagine that a pilot sitting with his wife in first class hadn't already seen off the better part of a bottle of *Chateauneuf du Pape*. He couldn't help and we wouldn't be able to fly on to the US after this diversion. Time was now pressing and the onward plan would have to wait.

It was at this point that Penny came out of the loo. She gave me a quizzical look and went back to her seat.

Time to refocus on the job at hand. Passengers briefed, fuel dumped, approach and landing made. It was now dark. We were instructed to taxi to a remote part of the airport because the main terminal was ill equipped to deal with such a large aircraft. It quickly became apparent that the whole airport was not used to dealing with such a large aircraft.

We were guided to our parking position by a baton-wielding marshaller. I noticed there was a traffic cone on the tarmac to our left which I thought was close, but not too close to become an issue. The marshaller seemed to think otherwise because he left his safe position on our nose and started running towards the cone, presumably intending to move it out of our way. His line of travel was taking him closer and closer to the danger zone of our left engine. He was plainly unaware how powerful these large engines were, even at idle power, and there was a real danger he was going to be sucked into it. I jammed on the brakes, reached for the left engine shutoff switch and closed the engine down, hoping I'd done it quickly enough not to have a tragedy on our hands.

I still wonder if he realises how close he was to becoming a mess of blood and bone. After the event, and with particularly black humour, Tim referred to the marshaller as potential FOD (foreigner object damage).

The ambulance team carried the now unconscious passenger from the aircraft, which concluded my part in the lady's clearly very sad story.

Company operations had made the decision that it would be best to fly back to Heathrow, accommodate the rest of the passengers there for the night and start again the next day. A slight complication was that the refueller didn't know how to refuel our aircraft, and there was no engineer licensed to do the required checks on the aircraft. As captain, I was granted a one-off authorisation to carry out the checks, which was fine, but I'd never done them before either, and so they took me quite a while. I really, really wanted to get it right!

At three o'clock in the morning we finally arrived back at Heathrow, having done a rather large round robin trip.

I'm afraid I never managed to find out if the lady survived. I hope she did. I hope she is OK.

A Bit at a Time

It's very rare for any flight to start with the aircraft's fuel tanks anywhere near full. We have a sophisticated and complex flight planning program that analyses every flight and calculates, to the nearest thimble full, the fuel required to complete it. It uses rolling three-month historical data on taxi out times, not just at each airport, but for each specific scheduled flight departure to calculate the fuel required to taxi out to the take-off position.

It then calculates the fuel required to climb, cruise and descend on the route, using the most economical levels for the expected aircraft weight, wind speeds and temperature conditions. Next, it calculates the fuel that would be required to complete the approach, and carry out a go around and divert to a nominated alternate airfield should it not be possible to land at the planned destination. It allows a small percentage on top of that for unknown variations and finally gives thirty minutes reserve fuel for good measure.

All this is known as the total 'trip fuel' and on the 777, flying a typical twelve-hour route from Shanghai to Heathrow this can be an eye watering 100 tonnes. A while back, aviation fuel was £700 a tonne, making this flight's fuel bill £70,000, so it makes sense to fine-tune the amount of fuel carried.

The heavier the aircraft, the harder the engines have to work, and this is turn imposes a greater restriction on the maximum achievable altitude. All this contributes to the aircraft being less efficient. Taking extra fuel obviously increases the weight of the aircraft. Due to this extra burden, 4% per hour of this fuel is burnt just to carry it. So, for a typical ten-hour flight, that 4% per hour swells to 40% over the whole trip, meaning that for every extra ton of fuel carried, 400 kg is burnt just to carry it. And that's expensive, a waste of resources and needlessly polluting.

However, that doesn't mean to say that we never carry extra, and it is ultimately up to the captain to decide on the fuel load. It makes sense to use experience and professional judgement to out-reason this scientific program if, for example, severe weather is anticipated anywhere along the route. Deviating hundreds of miles to avoid thunderstorms, or holding for a significant amount of time at a fog bound airport is never factored in by this program. So, I would never just go along with the calculated fuel figure without thinking it through first. And to be fair, the company never complained about any of my fuel decisions. Safety always comes first. But it's the unforeseen, out of the blue occurrences, that can sometimes make life difficult.

We were flying to Orlando where everything pointed to a normal day with good weather along the entire route; a glorious, settled day in Florida, and no expected delays. We could see no reason to take anything over the recommended calculated fuel figure.

As previously mentioned, to cross the Atlantic safely and efficiently, beyond conventional radar control, specific lanes or tracks are created to allow safe separation between aircraft. When our crossing clearance arrived, we were surprised that it was entirely different to the one we had planned and requested. It was a much longer route, a slower speed and a much lower altitude.

Regulations are complex but they state that, amongst other things, an aircraft must land with at least the reserve fuel figure remaining, representing thirty minutes flying time - for us roughly 3,000 kilogrammes of fuel. Inputting the new route information into our flight computer indicated that instead of our planned arrival fuel of 5,500 kilogrammes, we would arrive with 300 kilogrammes, i.e. with just four minutes flying time remaining before the engines wheezed their last. Clearly as things stood, we were unlikely to make it to Orlando.

Having only just begun the flight, we presently had loads of fuel, but it did mean that, legally, we had to nominate a closer airfield as our temporary destination.

We tried to renegotiate a new route or at least a different altitude or speed to make us more fuel efficient but it seemed that due to unforeseen circumstances every single permutation had already been taken. We couldn't climb because there was an aircraft at the next level, 1,000 feet above us, who was being blocked from climbing by a higher aircraft. Neither could we increase our speed because we risked catching up with the aircraft ahead of us. It seemed we had become the soggy lettuce stuffed limply into that day's Atlantic sandwich.

We were informed that some of the blocking aircraft would peel off the track system several hours ahead. That would allow us to climb, become more fuel efficient, and from there we could reassess. Until that happened, we moved along the route constantly looking at diversion airports where we could refuel.

For each airport, we calculated our arrival fuel - was it acceptable? Were the weather conditions within limits to make an approach and landing? Were the runways long enough, and was there engineering cover available to prepare the aircraft for the subsequent departure? Our passengers would have a long day, they would need more food and water, and could the airport supply it? It became like an ecclesiastical mantra for diverting pilots. Chris, the first officer, and I were working at a constant, intensive pace.

St John's, Newfoundland. Then Halifax, Nova Scotia. Then Bangor, Maine. Eventually we were cleared to climb to the next level, 1,000 feet above us, making us slightly more fuel efficient. OK, we could now make Boston. Another 1,000 feet climb. Again, we were a little more fuel efficient and we could now make New York. No, not New York, they couldn't accept us, they were too busy. OK, how about Newark, and then Philadelphia?

Next, we were allowed to accelerate to a more efficient speed. Bermuda was now in our sights. It felt as though Chris and I were in the ultimate reality game show where points made prizes, and our prize was being allowed to carry on towards Orlando.

One of the cabin crew came into the flight deck and brought us a cup of tea. He sat down on the jump-seat with a huff, and explained how awful and difficult his job was sometimes: 'We've run out of ice creams. We are about ten magnums short.'

I nodded in response, then turned to Chris and asked: 'can you check the weather for Bermuda?'

'I'm finding it all very stressful to be honest,' the cabin crew member continued.

'And can Bermuda accept us if needs be?' I added.

'And here you are, just sitting in your techno conservatory, in the sun, drinking tea.'

'Bermuda can accept us,' Chris reported.

'Honestly, you pilots don't know the half of it. Anyway, what's going on?'

'Well, at the moment we are planning on diverting to Bermuda.'

'What, to get ice cream?'

Chris spilled his tea.

We never got the chance to make the world's most expensive ice cream run because shortly after that we were given clearance to climb to our most economical cruising altitude and speed, and finally made it to Orlando.

It's Snowing in New York

It was snowing in New York and I knew it was going to be a long trip back home. Obviously, snow and aircraft don't get along very well. Although their effects are understood and can be taken into account, any form of freezing precipitation creates an extra layer of complication.

Freezing water entering the various probes and sensors can block vital information from reaching the instruments that, for example, show speed and height. To prevent this from happening, these probes and sensors are all fitted with heaters.

Even small amounts of snow or ice on the wings can very quickly turn aircraft into bricks. As it's not an exact science, the authorities make it easy for us: Before take-off, all snow and ice must be removed from the aircraft surface.

At JFK, this is normally achieved whilst on the parking stand. The aircraft is squirted with de-icing fluid, normally coloured either green or orange so everyone can see where it has been treated. Depending on the type of fluid, and the type and severity of the precipitation (wet snow, dry snow, freezing rain) it is possible to work out how long the de-icing fluid will be effective in preventing further frozen deposits.

The process of de-icing an aircraft is a finely balanced and often frustrating affair. Airport authorities will only put you in the queue to be de-iced once you are fully ready. That is, with all passengers on board, all cargo loaded, and all doors closed. There is often a very, very long queue for the de-icing rigs, and you can wait for hours. There are often not enough rigs, and considering the acreage of metal they have to de-ice, they frequently have to go back and replenish their supplies. Once the de-icing has taken place, pressure mounts for the pilots. The clock has started and you now have to organise pushback, taxi and take-off before the effectiveness of the de-icing fluid is so reduced that snow and ice start to accumulate on the wings again. Airports with snowy conditions often resemble extremely congested carparks. Arriving aircraft cannot get onto stand because they are still occupied by aircraft waiting for de-icing. Departing aircraft struggle through this cat's cradle of congestion trying to reach the take-off point.

Mixed in with all this, there are aeroplanes in the queue for take-off that have to return to stand because they have either run out of time and snow is starting to build up again, or they have been in the queue for so long their fuel reserves are below that required for the flight.

Overlaying this chaos, there is JFK's unique take on controlling. They are very busy and very good, but they work on the principle of, 'why say one word when ten words will do'. It doesn't matter to them that many foreign pilots will be a little weary, having just completed a ten-hour flight, landed on a slippery runway in near white-out conditions, and are now trying their best to cope with a stream of instructions lobbed at them in their second language with Bronx top spin:

'Callsign. We told you to wait at holding point Delta. You've gone too far. Why did you go too far? Now you will have to wait for the 737 to pass on your right and then turn right onto taxiway foxtrot, do a 180 at Juliet, recite the entire works of Shakespeare and then proceed as previously instructed.' I could imagine the scene inside the flight deck because I've been there myself:

The captain applies the brakes, sighs wearily and asks: 'What did he say?'

First officer: 'No idea. Shall we wait till he stops shouting at us and ask him to repeat?'

At Heathrow the same instruction would be as follows: 'Callsign, hold position for a moment'.

Anyway, to return to that snowy day at JFK. Whilst waiting for the de-icing rigs to arrive, I calculated our maximum allowable duty time, and by the same reckoning, the latest time we could push back from the stand to reach London before we all turned into mice and pumpkins. As yet, it was a disconcertingly long way off.

I conveyed this to the senior cabin crew member who was surprisingly on board with it all. They were a great crew but I couldn't help thinking that very soon they would start earning overtime at a rate similar to the gross domestic product of a smallish dictatorship. That had got to help.

Against the odds, it all worked out. As we began our climb after take-off, I looked at the clock and realised that, by coincidence, it was exactly the same time as our scheduled arrival time at London.

But instead of being very tired and about to drive home, we were very tired and only just starting the flight with an arrival time seven hours away.

Getting on a Bit

Crews going into China have to be extra diligent and ensure their immigration paperwork is filled out correctly. The collection of the data is normally delegated to the cabin manager, and so halfway through the flight we let her into the flight deck to start the process. I gave her my passport, which was nearing the end of its ten-year lifespan. I could see her looking at it and musing on something, so I asked her what was wrong. She turned the passport towards me, opened at the photograph page.

'What happened to you?' she asked.

And that got me thinking. Every time I go through US Immigration, I have my photograph taken, and I've been to America a lot over the last thirty years. I wonder if it would be possible to collate all those photographs into a single back catalogue. I could then replay them like one of those animated flip books. It would be like watching the Wicked Witch of the East who, having lost the elixir of eternal youth, rapidly grew more and more decrepit until finally collapsing in a pile of rotting flesh and bones. Look what half a lifetime of jet lag and nights out of bed can do to you. What a great retirement present that would be.

More ridiculously, I was having a drink with the crew in Washington recently. After I had ordered a beer, I was asked to show some ID. 'You have got to be kidding!' I said. 'Look at me, I'm practically Neolithic. Out of all the people in this group, you really think it's me who might be under age?'

Look at the Size of it

Airport security is patently of the utmost importance and I would be the last person to want it relaxed. However, what is deemed acceptable does have variations on a theme from country to country.

The first officer and I were going through security in Japan. The diligent security staff pulled me aside for a bag rummage. They had spotted something they were not happy about. Thank goodness they were wearing gloves, because they spent several minutes scrabbling around in the detritus that was my flight bag. I thought they may well have discovered a new form of life, perfectly adapted to fusty darkness and able to survive on biscuit crumbs and bits of cheese.

Eventually, they found their quarry. It was my Swiss Army accessory. I'm loathe to call it a knife because the entire thing was only three centimetres long and the blade was even shorter. It had been a gift from my father-in-law, and I loved it. It was exquisitely made and, in Swiss Army knife tradition, its tiny accessories had proved incredibly useful for almost a decade.

It had travelled everywhere with me, and it had never caused an issue. Not today though. They weren't going to allow me to enter the airport with it. Fair enough. Rule are rules, but I was incredulous when right next to me the first officer was repacking his four-cell Maglite torch - a cosh-like piece of metal nearly forty centimetres long and weighing in at more than a kilogram. It looked so deadly,

I'm sure he could have single-handedly kept Eric Blood-Axe and his entire army at bay during one of their shopping trips to Northumberland.

It certainly made my tiny gadget pale into insignificance. But I wasn't about to let them confiscate it; it had too much sentimental value, so I asked one of our ground staff to take it back to check-in and put it in the hold.

As I walked out into the terminal, from the depths of my flight bag, I thought I heard Stilton, my cheese-based companion, breathe a sigh of relief.

I Say Tomato, You Say Tomaydo

Trying to while away a couple of hours during my short stay in Houston, Texas. The hotel was out of town, next to a ten-lane highway, and so the possibilities for sightseeing were limited.

The hotel didn't have a swimming pool; it had an arrangement with the local fitness centre instead. When I arrived there, I noticed what looked like half a dozen 'Walking Dead' extras all trying, and potentially failing, to stay afloat. I decided not to bother.

If in doubt, look at tools, so I went to Walmart and spent a happy hour gazing at all things manly. And America really knows how to do manly tools.

Outside it was hot and humid so I decided to give the rest of the sights a miss. Dunkin' Doughnuts and the local carpet warehouse would have to wait until my next visit. It was now approaching lunchtime so I thought I'd grab a sandwich and go back to the hotel. The delicatessen was empty except for the two blokes behind the counter. Images of the film Deliverance and being made to 'squeal like a pig' flashed through my mind but then some office workers arrived and the place instantly felt more civilised.

This was America's Deep South and accents were quite thick. So when I ordered a tuna roll with lettuce, tomato, and spinach, the sandwich maker (deputy vice president) put spinach in the bread roll and then looked at me blankly. I repeated 'tomato and lettuce' and received another blank stare. I pointed at the container of tomatoes but my aim must have been off because it yielded no response. I was desperately trying to think of a way of miming a tomato when one of the friendly office workers translated and said, 'Give him laydus and tomeydoe.'

I thanked her and moved along to pay.

The second big bloke asked me, 'What you git?'

'A six inch tuna sub roll'.

'A wat?'

'A six inch tuna sub', I replied, annunciating as best I could.

Blank stares again. Dear God, if this carries on, I'm going to starve to death. 'I'm sorry, I don't know what else to tell you. You were standing right next to your colleague when he made my sandwich.'

More blank stares because what he probably heard was, 'mew spew blah blah fink splodge.'

The friendly office worker rescued me for a second time: 'He's got 'too-na.'

That's Got to Hurt

We had night stopped in the US and were on the bus on our way back to the airport, when I overheard a surprising conversation between two cabin crew ladies. They were talking about summer holidays. (In fairness I should stress that multiple trips involving jet lag and nights out of bed can start to have an effect on reasoning.)

'I saw this lovely bikini in the mall. Tried it on. It was so small it hurt, but it was really lovely and I just had to have it.'

'Didn't you try a bigger size?'

'No. I was so tired I wanted to go to bed, so I just bought that one.'

A third lady joined the conversation: 'I've been shopping and I have a suitcase full of stuff. And the ridiculous thing is, I don't even like most of it, and I know for a fact that I could have got most of it cheaper in the UK.'

I too have experienced jet lag-based consumerism. With just twenty-four hours off in New York, I had been sent on a mission to buy my daughter some clothes from Abercrombie and Fitch. As far as my body was concerned it was the early hours of the morning. As I approached the store, I realised I was tired because the world was shifting in shuddering jolts as if a camera was rapidly zooming in and out. I also realised the shop was evidently not intended to cater for my generation - it had the appearance of a nightclub, and the moment I stepped inside, I felt as if I was trespassing.

It was very dark which I thought strange for a shop selling clothes. Perhaps you were supposed to select items by smell. To complete the club vibe, loud music was bellowing out with a thumping baseline and repetitive lyrics, something along the lines of, *'it is what it is, it is what it isn't, it is what it is, it is what it isn't.'* On and on. I found my tired brain synchronising with it, and I began to stagger around in time with the ninety-beat cadence, like a DJ rapper way beyond his sell by date.

The store was full of beautiful young people who contrasted alarmingly with me. The five o'clock shadow, sunken black-ringed eyes, and the haunted expression of a man literally old enough to be their father. I started to feel like a vagrant who had wandered in off the street seeking warmth. Staggering around blindly, by some miracle I managed to find a pair of trousers I thought my daughter would like. But what size? No idea. I looked around for someone to help me, but it was difficult to spot an assistant when surrounded by so much youth.

What to do? Should I stare at someone and then smile when I caught their eye? But what if they were just another shopper? I imagined the news headlines the next day: 'Man arrested for lewd behaviour in Abercrombie and Fitch', followed by an eye witness statement from Brady: 'I thought he was a pervert.'

Maybe try a different approach? And then I was saved. A young lady with a name tag approached me: 'Hi' ...*it is what it is...* 'Kimber' ...*what it isn't...* 'do you' ...*it is what it is...* 'help?'

Normally in a loud social situation I would just smile inanely and nod at what I hoped was the right time, but this wasn't a social setting and it would have looked weird to grin haplessly at this young lady. I guessed she was called Kimberly, because that's what it said on her name tag, and I was pretty sure I'd heard her say the word 'help'. Either she wanted to help me or she was informing me she had just called for help from security. I went with the former. I shouted I was trying to buy something for my daughter who was a similar size to her. Could she help me with the sizing?

'Oh sure. I'm super small.'

Who would have thought that in a country with 'all you can eat' buffets and supersized meals, there would be such a thing as 'super small?'

Take Care

As I've mentioned previously, crews constantly taking anti-malarial medication suffered from stomach problems, mouth ulcers, and headaches. The side-effects were so unpleasant, most crews just stopped taking the medication. The airline's latest approach to malaria prevention is much kinder. Doctors and risk assessors agreed that if crews were accommodated in air-conditioned hotels in cities, places with a low risk of malarial infection, new guidelines could be issued. They included not going outdoors between the hours of darkness; wearing light, long sleeved shirts and long trousers; and using effective repellents like DEET. If all these guidelines were followed then crews did not need to take anti-malarial pills. *

This was great news as it meant we would no longer be diarrhoea-desiccated husks. Of course, it also required a more sensible and grown-up approach to our own healthcare. It surprised me therefore that I often saw crew members, mainly the invincible young ones, meeting up by the hotel pool for a few beers to watch the African sunset. If there is a perfect time to guarantee being bitten by mosquitoes, it is at sunset. Tragically, crews *have* contracted malaria and some have died from it too.

So you can imagine my concern when, having arrived home from a trip, I started to feel poorly with a high temperature, shivers, headaches, muscle pains and diarrhoea. Oh, and I'd been to Africa the week before. The doctor told me to go to the hospital.

'I've been sent for a blood test for possible malaria,' I said to the receptionist.

I could have fired a starting pistol at the world championship 100m sprint and achieved the same effect: She stood up so quickly her chair went flying across the room and, in a blur of motion, she was eyeing me from behind the filing cabinet.

'I can't give you malaria even if I have it,' I said through clenched teeth and clenched buttocks, trying to reassure her that her HAZMAT suit wasn't going to be necessary. Well, if the clenched buttocks didn't work, maybe it would be.

A few anxious days were spent waiting for the results. I kept myself amused by turning myself inside out on the toilet. It transpired that I didn't have malaria but I had gone down with Salmonella poisoning. So that was alright then.

* I must point out that this advice is for crews who are staying for short periods in and around their accommodation. Most people visiting Africa have a different agenda from sunning themselves by the hotel pool for a day and should therefore seek proper medical advice.

On Time

US shopping malls are worlds where supersizing and excess are king (sized). I saw an advert which proclaimed, 'Buy two watches, get three more free.'

What sort of messed up world is that, I wondered. Who could possibly want or need five watches? I imagined myself walking through the airport terminal shouting, 'Ho,

Ho, Ho, Merry Watchmass', and throwing watches around like rice at a wedding.

'Look mommy, it's Pilot Watchmass, can I have one?'

'No honey, we already have five watches each.'

Know When You're Beaten

Preparing for departure in the Middle East we were listening on ground control frequency to the following conversation between a local aircraft (his callsign K12) and ground control (GC):

K12: 'Ground, this is Kilo12, requesting security to the aircraft.'

GC: 'Confirm you want security?'

K12: 'Oh yes'. After a few minutes...

GC: 'K12 can you say the reason for wanting security?'

K12: 'There is a passenger on the aircraft and he is smoking and it is not allowed. The cabin crew have tried to stop him but he is fighting with them.'

After a few more minutes....

K12: 'He is fighting with the ground staff now.'

GC: 'Roger, the security team are on the way.'

And a few more minutes pass...

K12: 'He is now fighting with the security men, but of course they are winning very well indeed.'

That incident reminds me of the time we were flying to Jamaica on the TriStar. One of the passengers had become so abusive and threatening that the captain had authorised the use of the restraint kit. With the help of the engineer (who else?) and some hefty passengers, this large, aggressive man was subdued and secured in his seat.

We had all settled back into our routine when a further call came in from the crew. They were now having difficulty with another passenger. The mother of Mr Aggressive was so embarrassed at the shame his behaviour had brought upon their family, that she had set on him. Restrained and totally defenceless, he was being berated by this feisty lady, and repeatedly beaten over the head with her handbag.

Sometimes It's The Simplest Things

If you've ever flown, you will have heard the pre-take-off and landing announcements, instructing you to ensure that your seat belt is fastened, the seat back table stowed and your seat is in the upright position. All done, of course, to put you and your immediate surroundings in the safest possible configuration for these safety critical parts of the flight.

In a large section of the aircraft, when your seat is reclined, it encroaches on the space of the passenger in the row behind, and this prevents them from adopting the safety bracing position during an emergency. Emergency breaking on the runway is very efficient these days, and if you weren't strapped into your seat you would most likely end up sprawled on the floor some distance away, probably wearing the toupee and false teeth of the person sitting behind you.

The crew tell us when the cabin is 'secure' for take-off and we can't depart until this has happened. And next time you are on an aircraft, listen out for a series of chimes just before we enter the runway. This confirms their message has been received and we are about to depart.

Sometimes, we reach the front of the queue for departure, and the cabin is not fully ready. We allow the use of the in-flight entertainment system during our taxi out, but it is interrupted to show the safety demonstration. And this interruption was presumably the final straw in a little boy's already stressful day. CBeebies had vanished off his screen and for him this was totally unacceptable. He had a full-blown Basil Faulty melt down, stormed out of his seat and started to run around the cabin screaming his head off. Perhaps most of us feel like that most of the time but maturity stops us from acting on it (most of the time).

The crew tried reasoning with him but he was having none of it. Every time they approached him, he ran off bawling at the top of his voice. His parents were the type who would have told Vlad the Impaler he was being a little unreasonable whilst he did unspeakable things to his enemies. The crew asked them to help but they were so ineffectual it was a wonder they had managed to get dressed that morning.

We had blocked the flow of traffic for departure so air traffic control moved us out of the way, and we were now facing a further dilemma. The queue to the take-off point had already been longer than expected, and with this extra enforced delay we were eating into our fuel reserves and fast approaching our go/no go point.

I sent a message back to explain to the parents that if we didn't depart in the next five minutes we would have to return to stand for more fuel, and we would also have to think very carefully whether it was going to be acceptable for them to continue their journey with us.

Still nothing from them apart from a non-committal grimace and something about their son being 'a bit headstrong at times'. Absolutely no sign of them troubling themselves to get out of their seats and talk to their son. Then one of the female crew members, who was about ten feet away from the wailing little chap, crouched down and said to him, 'Do you want a hug?'

He looked at her dubiously for a few moments and then said, 'Yes'.

He ran into her arms, and with that, she picked him up and popped him back into his seat! 'We're going to blast off into the sky in a minute. Won't that be exciting?'

Nod.

'And a soon as I can, I'll come and put some cartoons on for you. Will that be OK?'

Nod.

We told the parents we couldn't afford a repeat performance. We simply didn't have the fuel reserves to hold while they persuaded him into his seat for landing.

Luckily, he behaved.

Probably because we arranged for CBeebies to be replayed just before landing.

Snot the Way to Behave

The weather in Shanghai was terrible; heavy rain and high winds. I normally plan on doing something new on each of my visits, but on that day I accepted defeat. The hotel had a lovely, large indoor swimming pool, so I decided to go for a swim. A friendly receptionist welcomed me into the health suite with much bowing and scraping and a fanfare just falling short of full ceremonial trumpets and fireworks.

'Hello sir, you want a swim?'

'Yes, please, I want a swim.'

'Okay, you have signed book now, you can go for swim.'

So off I went towards the changing rooms. I was a little confused, what with the weather being so awful, because I seemed to have a shadow. I soon realised it wasn't actually a shadow but the receptionist who had, with military precision, fallen into step with me, clutching a towel. He then broke formation and raced ahead to open the changing room door for me. I don't know about you, but I always get very uncomfortable when people show signs of subservience. I don't want it, certainly don't need it, and I never know what to do. We ended up standing there both saying, 'thank you, thank you' in unison. We had become two nodding Churchill dogs on the parcel shelf of a car.

'This can't go on for much longer,' I thought to myself, desperately trying to come up with a way to break the deadlock.

He must have been thinking on similar lines, because he rushed forward and beckoned me to an empty changing cubicle. He stood there, ramrod straight, with the towel draped over his arm. As you know from a previous episode, I'm quite a prude when it comes to showing my bits to total strangers, so I took the towel from him and made it clear I could manage on my own.

'No, I stay.'

'No, you go,' I insisted.

Reluctantly, he went.

So, into the swimming pool. I swim with a waterproof MP3 music player. I had the pool to myself and I soon settled into a relaxed rhythm, enjoying both the swimming and the music.

About twenty minutes in, I was joined by a would-be local alpha-male in speedos. I could tell he meant business because to announce his arrival he stood on the poolside and made a point of executing some rather exaggerated stretches. He then got into the water and with a flourish, immediately started pounding down the pool at great speed, only to come to a gasping halt at the other end.

He looked over to make sure I'd noticed him (how could I not?) and then set off again with great gusto, storming down the pool before once again coming to a spluttering halt. To my astonishment, he then started to pick his nose and, having excavated it, inspected his work with interest. Next, he cleared his nasal passages by sucking air noisily through his nose and coughing the scavenged goodies back into his mouth. He then spat the whole lot into the swimming pool.

Suddenly I wasn't enjoying my swim any more. I also started to notice that the pool wasn't quite as clean as I had first thought. Was that plankton misting the water? Oh, look, perhaps a jellyfish! No, it was the inner workings of this kind gentleman.

To seal the deal, he came up with an even more efficient and disgusting method of nasal cleansing. Blocking one nostril with a finger, he blew out hard through the other. He seemed very pleased with the result.

I quickly decided to get out of the pool, shuddering at the thought of what I might have to wash out of my hair.

Only in Jamaica

On the way to the hotel in Kingston, I overheard two crew members talking about trips they enjoyed. One said, 'Here, in Jamaica. I hire a car and drive into the Blue Mountains to buy coffee. It's the best coffee I've ever had and it's half the price I'd pay in the UK.'

The other replied, 'I guess hiring a car for £60 to get the coffee probably makes it slightly more expensive than in the UK?'

Long silence, and then, 'Mmm, I guess you are right'.

On arrival at the hotel, I was amused to see a sign in my bathroom that read: 'Guests are kindly requested not to bring Ganga into their rooms.'

For Better or Worse

In the brochures, a far away, exotic wedding looks incredibly romantic and idyllic. But if it's going to be the day you dreamed of, you need to make some careful choices, because I've seen it go wrong many times.

You will have travelled thousands of miles and through many time zones and will probably be feeling a bit worse for wear because of it. Jet lag and wedding nerves do not make good companions, so it's worth taking the time to acclimatise.

You will need to allow for the fact that you may have left most of your friends behind because they couldn't afford the journey. And those that *have* travelled may be slightly miffed at having to splash out on what is, effectively, someone else's holiday.

I've seen Cinderella wedding gowns for the bride, and heavy suits, or Scottish kilts and long socks for the groom. All very stylish, but don't forget you'll be standing in 34°C heat and nearly 100% humidity, in full sun. If you dress like that, expect to be saying your vows drenched in your own bodily fluids. And please do your homework. That romantic wedding arch shown in the brochure, looking out over the azure, calm, tropical sea could, in reality, be right by the main pool or the main beach. Both are public areas. During the ceremony you can almost guarantee there will be a man just a few meters away wearing nothing but a banana hammock and sporting burnt back boobs, clutching his free all-inclusive pint and leering at the bridesmaids.

With the ceremony over, you can look forward to your honeymoon but don't forget you may be sharing it with a mother-in-law you don't get on with, and a few surly friends who would probably rather not be there.

Either that, or it will be a dream come true.

That Samba Right Mess
You've Got Yourself Into

Many pilots organise their flying trips around their interests and hobbies. Some captains follow the Formula One season around the world, others the major tennis tournaments. Some choose their destinations by the quality of the golf courses and to some extent I often chose diving destinations. In my view, if you have to be somewhere it might as well be the Maldives or Mauritius.

On the whole, though, I wasn't sufficiently organised to fine tune my trips, and it would often be a case of finding out what was going on when I arrived. This lucky dip approach has led to some great surprises. For example, arriving in New York in time to watch their fantastic Greenwich Village Halloween Parade, or Hong Kong for their Chinese New Year celebrations, or arriving home on my wedding anniversary. Well, OK, I planned that last one.

So, I arrived in Rio de Janeiro and apparently it was carnival week. It seemed strange nobody had actually planned to operate this flight to see it. The crew were very excited at the prospect of witnessing this world-famous spectacle, so I thought we could find a street in the city centre and watch the parade. I asked the concierge for more information and I couldn't have been more behind the times if I'd stood in front of him wearing tartan trews singing 'Bye Bye Baby' by the Bay City Rollers. Since way back in 1984, when the parade had seemingly become too big for its platform boots, it has been held in a purpose-built stadium called the Sambadrome. And unless we had tickets, we were not going to see a thing, and they had sold out months ago. Maybe it wasn't such a fluke I was there after all.

The concierge suggested we go and have a look at one of the many *blocos* in the city, as they were considered the heart and soul of the Rio Carnival. He explained *blocos* were casual street parties run by local groups. There was dancing and local percussion music throughout the day and often into the early hours of the morning. One of the oldest *blocos*, *Monobloco*, holds its party on Copacabana Beach and I was told up to 80,000 revellers take part.

My crew were predominantly very young, average age twenty-one. I was literally old enough to be their father. I've noticed that young crew generally split into two groups. Group one is fiercely confident and independent, and group two, a little reticent and reserved - a trait which can be a lifesaver in some parts of the world. A female crew member, who was definitely in group one, had gone to a nightclub the night before, and then accepted an invite back to the house of a local man. She had gone on her own, not told anyone where she was going or when she was expecting to be back, and by all accounts, she had a great time. So she couldn't understand why we were surprised she had actually made it back at all.

A few weeks earlier one of our first officers had been robbed at knife point, in broad daylight, just outside our crew hotel. Ironic, as the hotel, right on the sea front, was chosen because it was purportedly in one of the safest districts. Of course, all large cities demand a certain amount of caution and respect, and parts of Rio come with warning bells, red flags and flashing neon lights.

Perhaps with this is mind, the crew in 'group two' were keen on the idea of going to see the festivities but a little nervous about the practicalities. Tom and Phil, the first officers, and I offered to organise and chaperone a trip to Copacabana the next day.

In my experience, few locals in Rio speak English. Even shouting in that slow, deliberate way we adopt in foreign climes didn't really work. But, as we boarded the bus for the forty-minute ride into town, a deliberate 'Copa ca bana, por favor', seemed to do the trick. My linguistic skills were evidently improving and I tried not to look too pleased with myself as the door closed and we set off to - as it happened - not quite Copacabana.

We were deposited at the closest stop to the beach, which was in a back street about half a mile from the beach itself. The crew gathered like chicks around a mother hen (me). I found my bearings and we set off on what I'm sure would have been a lovely walk if the refuse collectors had been before us; if it hadn't been 35°C in the shade, and if the young'uns, who were expecting a party, hadn't come dressed in posh frocks and very high heels.

As we walked, my mind drifted to the last time I was here, with Pen. Together we had visited Rio's most iconic sites, Sugarloaf Mountain and the statue of Christ the Redeemer. I'd wanted to go up Sugarloaf Mountain since 1979 when it was featured in a ridiculous fight scene in the film Moonraker, and if you ever get the chance to take the cable car journey up to the top, I would highly recommend it. The views are almost otherworldly. It takes a while for your brain to process the monolithic granite mountains rising out of the sea; the white sand beaches backed by the high mountains of the Tijuca National Park and, in the distance, perched on the sheer edge of the massive Corcovado Mountain, the majestic statue of Christ the Redeemer.

Access to the statue is via a twisting, turning tramway that climbs through a dense, jungle landscape. It is a magical journey, a perfect precursor to what lies ahead. Christ the Redeemer stands at thirty-eight meters and weighs over six hundred tonnes. With arms outstretched, it gazes out over the city of Rio de Janeiro, emanating a palpable aura of peace and compassion. It has been voted one of the seven wonders of the modern world and it's not hard to understand why. It is a humbling experience to be in the presence of something that, although composed of concrete and soapstone, exudes so much spirituality. And its setting is glorious.

My reverie of past visits to Rio was interrupted by a shrill cry from one of the crew: 'Oh my God I've just trodden in a dead rat!'

'Eeeew', gasped another.

This was followed by lots more screaming and shouting and running around, and flapping arms. Lots of 'oh, my God' and 'gross', and 'I think I'm going to be sick'. One of the crew said 'oh, poor thing', and I wasn't sure if she was referring to the dead creature, or the person with liquified rat oozing between her toes. Some semblance of order was restored when one of her quick-thinking friends poured a bottle of water over her foot.

Finally, we all burst out onto Copacabana feeling somewhat hot and bothered. This world-famous beach is, well, just a beach really. It's two and a half miles long, and the western end has magnificent views of the aforementioned Sugarloaf Mountain. There are many beach shacks and an imposing promenade, but it also backs onto a six-lane highway, and tall, faceless hotel and apartment blocks.

We spotted the party bus where presumably a band would be doing its thing. There were a handful of sound engineers 'one-two-one-two-ing' into microphones, but very little else. People were milling around as if expecting something to happen but after about twenty minutes loitering in the glaring sun, nothing continued to happen. The crew were becoming increasingly fractious, thirsty and in need of the loo, and they kept looking at me as if expecting I would conjure up a Samba band, bejewelled dancers and 80,000 party goers.

The best I could do was find some shade at one of the beach cafes, direct them to the toilets and order drinks. However, they were expecting a festival and they hadn't been given a festival, and they soon became bored. I suggested a swim but they hadn't brought their swimming things, and anyway they said it would mess with their makeup.

There were still people milling around with hopeful looks on their faces but honestly, I had seen more people queueing up at our local 'Big Tasty' kebab shack. Seeing an opportunity, a busker arrived, set up shop and began playing his guitar. The small crowd, eager to be entertained, soon started to clap and sing along but it was like going to the Formula One Grand Prix at Silverstone and watching the valet parking guys instead of the race.

'Well, this sucks,' one of the crew announced.

'We're like hot and miserable and want to go back to the hotel,' said another. 'Thing is, we weren't paying attention to the route so we have no idea how to get back. Will you take us?' I cursed the concierge's misinformation. It looked as if it would be hours before anything remotely interesting was going to happen, so I agreed to take them back. 'And can we get ice cream on the way?' pleaded one of the crew.

'Yes, we can get ice cream.'

The next day, determined to salvage something from this trip, Phil and I decided to go cycling in the hills behind the hotel, using bikes hired from the Flying Staff Recreation Club. Many years ago, an enterprising pilot decided he would start the scheme, and we are privileged to have access to it. For a very modest subscription, the club obtains membership for local gyms, squash, tennis, golf and health clubs all around the world. We also have access to bikes, kite boards, sailing dinghies, surfboards, windsurfers and snorkelling equipment.

In this case though, we were in two minds about whether to bother because, although they were mid-range road bikes, they were fast approaching the end of their useful life. Rusty chains, gears faltering, saddles well-worn - all in all, they were in a bit of a state. We took a puncture repair kit with us just in case. About an hour into the ride, we passed a man and his trestle table piled high with papaya and other exotic-looking fruit. Fatigued from the hill climb, we stopped for a breather and a glass of his home-made papaya-based smoothie.

As we sat there enjoying the stunning view, a battered old car came around the corner. We were warned of its approach several minutes in advance, thanks to the booming rap music that accompanied it. Its four occupants were young, sullen, and had an air of menace. Each of them had a tattooed arm hanging limply out of the car's open windows and there were enough rings, bling and bangles on display to rival the Crown Jewels.

One was swaying his head far too slowly to match any beat from the frantic cacophony blasting out of the windows. Maybe he was secretly listening to Tchaikovsky on his ear buds. Probably not.

We waved casually, trying to look harmless and friendly, like you would if the school alpha bully walks past at playtime. They stared at us aggressively as they drove by. And then the car slowed, stopped, and turned around.

Shit. Shit. Shit.

When I'm out and about in certain counties I never wear my watch because it attracts too much attention. Instead, I have a £10 digital, no wedding ring, no credit cards, and just enough local cash and a few US dollars to hopefully satisfy a would-be mugger. I was beginning to hope I had brought enough for four. The car cruised past us again, its passengers eyeballing the bikes. They stopped and one of the rear passengers, the one not listening to Tchaikovsky, got out, still eyeballing the bikes.

I whispered to Tom beseechingly, 'He's looking at the bikes, do you think he's interested in cycling?'

At that moment, the man lifted up his T-shirt to reveal, not only more nasty looking tattoos, but also a handgun stuffed into the waistband of his shorts. I couldn't compete with that because I was a '*mamil*' (middle aged man in lycra), and had nothing in my shorts apart from the obvious, and they had retreated so far into my body I probably had a camel toe. I suddenly wished we were back at Copacabana beach not listening to Samba, not partying and also not being shot in the head for a couple of poxy bikes.

The fruit seller must have suddenly remembered he'd left his washing out because I realised he had silently slunk off into the woods.

'*Bom Dia*', I said, hoping that, for once, I was using the right language. They speak Portuguese in Brazil and the Span-glish hybrid nonsense I usually end up spouting really wasn't going to go down well in this situation.

The man with the hand-gun didn't respond but stared at us through lazy eyelids. I thought he was probably trying to decide whether to shoot us and then take the bikes, or make us load the bikes into the car boot first and then shoot us. Personally, I would have opted for the latter as it would be a much more efficient way of doing things. He turned his attention to the bikes, was silent for quite some time, and then slowly moved his right-hand to his waist-band.

'This is it,' I thought. 'We're gonners.'

Suddenly, he let out the loudest laugh I have ever heard. We almost jumped out of our skins. I can only presume the bikes were in such a state he couldn't even be bothered to kill us.

As he stalked back to the car in that simian strut gangsters have, I thought I might be sick. After they had cruised off leaving a trail of rap behind them, Tom said shakily, 'Shall we go back to the hotel?'

'Yes', I replied, 'and can we get ice cream?'

A Blistering Tale

Nearing Antigua I was in the forward galley stretching my legs, having a cup of tea and talking to the cabin crew member who was responsible for running the galley.

She had her back to the ovens, and over her shoulder I noticed what appeared to be steam rising from one of the beverage makers. However, it soon became obvious it was actually a plume of smoke, growing thicker and darker by the second.

'We have a fire,' I said, pointing over her shoulder.

She glanced behind her, wide eyed. Reacting quickly, she dived for the electrical control panel and pulled the circuit breakers to isolate the power. Then she turned back to me and said, 'That could've been nasty'.

'Still is,' I replied, nodding at the black smoke still billowing from the 'bev' maker.

'Use the emergency power off switch,' I added, gesturing towards the big, red, guarded switch on the panel.

Meanwhile, I fetched a BCF fire extinguisher* and squirted the gaps in and around the appliance. And then we waited nervously to see if our efforts had produced the desired effect. Luckily, the smoke dissipated and we didn't have to launched into full firefighting procedures.

And that was that. It was all over in a matter of minutes. I mention it because the incident was typical of the job. We are often required to go from a relaxed and controlled state, to one where immediate, corrective action is required in order to avoid a situation quickly becoming catastrophic.

An hour later and grateful to be on the ground in Antigua, we watched the engineer remove the 'bev' maker appliance. The wiring cluster was damaged, which had caused sparking and subsequent burning of the electrical insulation.

You'll be pleased to hear there are many, many circuit breakers, switches and master power switches, mostly situated on the flight deck, that can be used to isolate pretty much every single electrical component on the aircraft. Everything, that is, apart from the kit that passengers bring onto the aeroplane. How many of us harumph at the cost of replacing a broken brand-named charger and opt instead for a cheap and nasty £1.99 generic charger bought from dodgy.com.

If it doesn't burst into flames itself, it could cause the lithium-ion batteries in your device to overheat and catch fire. Obviously in an aircraft you can't simply toss them out of the window, and thermal runaway on these batteries is a real and increasing problem. Crews are now required to undergo specialised training on how to deal with them.

Anyhow, off we went to the hotel, and a well-deserved beer. At that time, we were staying at The Hotel Marmite: inmates either loved it or hated it. It certainly wasn't a 'grande' or a 'deluxe'. Personally, I thought it didn't have a single redeeming quality. I'm sure that sounds very spoilt. We were staying in Antigua, for goodness sake. But it really was a horrible little place. Antigua is a shuttle destination. Crews arrive, have a night's rest in the hotel, and the following day fly a shuttle service from Antigua to another

Caribbean island, then back to Antigua for another night's rest. The hotel was so small it couldn't accommodate all the crews without some creative thinking, and the solution was to hotbed. For the shuttle service, crews were required to pack up their belongings, move out of their room and store their bags in a lock-up. As soon as the rooms were vacated, they were pounced upon by manic domestic staff who would feverishly clean them, ready for the next incoming crew. It was all done so quickly the new arrivals could almost feel the warmth of the previous occupant's body in their bed.

I don't know about you, but when I enter a hotel room, I like to pretend nobody else has used it. That's just not possible when the room has been cleaned so quickly there are dubious stains still visible on the carpet; someone else's pubic hair on the bathroom floor, and the bed is still fresh with the imprint of someone else's backside. Yes, but come on, we were in Antigua.

Watching your fingernails grow can often be marginally more interesting than watching TV in a foreign country. The Hotel Marmite, however, had a much better source of entertainment. The doors were so ill fitting that, more often than not, there would be a trail of carnivorous insects streaming relentlessly under the door, carrying deceased or paralysed prey to their home base somewhere at the other end of the room. It was like an unstoppable flow of lava and I was amazed at the variety of wildlife being dragged unwillingly across my floor. I imagined a subsequent visit where I entered my room and came across a crew member who had missed their wake-up call, been overlooked by the cleaning staff, and was now lying on the bed, stung into paralysis and being slowly dissected by the minuscule army, and then carried away bit by bit.

Whenever I visited the hotel, I always packed four shallow plastic bowls. Each bowl would be placed under a bed leg and filled with water. The nasty little buggers weren't going to chop me up in the middle of the night.

When I was a kid travelling around Europe with my parents, whenever we arrived at a new destination my father would always say 'What a bloody dump'. But after a good night's rest, the place would always seem much better. Hotel Marmite never got any better. For daytime relaxation you could either stew on a shade-less paving slab that masqueraded as the patio; cool down by breaking the crust of the fetid swimming pool, or walk the half mile down the hill to the beach.

'No sir, we don't provide a shuttle bus service to the beach. In fact, we don't provide a service for anything,' replied the receptionist to my enquiry.

She couldn't even be bothered to raise a smile. Maybe the previous evening's insects had had a go at her facial muscles, slowly softening her up for the big push later that night.

I'm not sure which of the leisure options was more depressing because the beach had no affiliation with the hotel. The first time I went down there, the crew, rather pitifully, showed me a pile of broken sun loungers piled up out of sight behind one of the drink shacks. Rejected by one of the more upmarket hotels, they were being heroically recycled by the crew.

I was down on the beach because I'd booked to go diving. I had a few minutes to spare, so I was cooling off by standing at the waterside, and watching the first officer water-skiing.

I was joined by one of the crew. 'What's he doing?' she asked.

For the briefest of moments, I was tempted to say the clue was surely in the fact that he was on the water and he had skis on his feet, but that would have been cruel and rude, so I just replied, 'He's tap dancing'.

No, I didn't say that either, because presumably she was just using one of the nonsensical conversation openers we Brits are famous for. A bit like the late Queen opening a new care home and asking one of its residents, 'Have you come far?'

The most striking part of her question was the accent with which it was delivered: Liverpudlian, so sharp you could etch glass with it. For such a small country I marvel at our huge range of accents. Even today, you need only go fifty miles up the road before you encounter an accent so thick it should probably come with subtitles. I'm a Lancashire lad and, at university, I lived in a student house with a Geordie and a Scotsman. Initially, our accents and quirky dialects were so pronounced that none of us could understand each other. But after nine pints on a Saturday night, it didn't seem to matter anymore. Anyway, back to Antigua. I woke the next morning having survived my in-house insect companions but, it seemed, not unscathed. My left ear and left wrist were itching like mad. Later that day, just before I went for my pre-flight rest, I noticed a slight blister on my wrist, and that my earlobe had swollen. Clearly, I'd been bitten, but not so badly that I wasn't fit to operate home.

During the flight however, things started to accelerate somewhat. Both my left ear and wrist became very swollen, so much so that the skin was unable to contain the build-up of fluid, and began to ooze. A kind and caring cabin crew member bandaged me up whilst I contacted the medical experts via our satellite phone. These guys are medical specialists who are available twenty-four hours a day for 'in air medical consultations'. I had used them many times for advice on passenger health issues, but never before about myself.

Before being handed over to a doctor, the operator followed her strict order of questions and it went something like this:

Q: Patient's name?   A: Nigel Knot.

Q: Patient's sex and age?   A: Male, 54.

Q: Flight details?   A: Antigua to London, presently mid Atlantic.

Q: Patient's symptoms?   A: Rapid and progressive blistering of left arm and left ear.

Q: Patient's seat number?   A: Flight deck, captain's seat.

Q: Oh. Er, hold the line, captain, I'll get a doctor.

We carry a comprehensive medical kit on board the aircraft, half of which can only be accessed by a medical practitioner. In my thirty years of airline flying, I have never said, 'if only there was a doctor on board'. Because, amazingly, there has always been at least one. Handy people these doctors. I'd love to know if there has ever been a situation in an operating theatre where the doctor has said, 'if only we had a pilot here'. Probably not - proving the point that we're not quite as handy to have around.

We were advised not to go delving too deeply into the onboard medical kit as I couldn't have anything intravenous and remain fit to operate. Instead, I could take a mix of antihistamine and anti-inflammatory medications. Unfortunately, neither seemed to work because, for the remainder of the flight, weeping blisters continued to erupt along both my arms.

For the next six weeks I transitioned from being an airline pilot to an object of medical fascination. The specialists couldn't decide whether I had picked up an infection from the dirty swimming pool, the diving trip, or an insect bite. Whatever the cause, they found it all very interesting. Every visit to the hospital saw my consultant inviting various onlookers ranging from medical students and infectious disease and dermatological specialists to fans of horror movies, to prod, poke, take notes, and photos. By that time both my arms, both legs and torso were completely covered in large, swollen and weeping blisters.

I had several small puncture holes as a result of skin biopsies to try and discover the nature of the problem, and I was pretty well covered head to foot in bandages. It was summer and I found it both easier and more comfortable to dress in shorts and tee shirt. Walking through the hospital during the visits to my consultant, I was always amused by the wide-eyed looks I received, as this seemingly animated mummy staggered along the corridors.

Slowly but surely, and a gallon of steroid cream later, the onslaught of blisters stopped and eventually dried up. This left me looking even worse, as the top layers of skin started to die and flake off like some hideous snake shedding its skin.

Despite the hotel's assurances that they had improved their anti-mosquito treatments and pool cleaning regime, I swore never to go back there again. But I have heard the Hotel Marmite has recently reimagined and rebranded itself as The Hotel Infectious Grande.

*Fires can only start and be maintained if the three elements of fuel, oxygen and a heat source exist together. (Sufficiently high temperatures can be enough to start a fire without an open flame or spark being present.) Removing any one of those elements will prevent a fire in the first place, or put one out if it has started. Water is the most obvious choice for firefighting as it is readily available, quickly reduces temperatures and goes some way to denying the fuel its necessary supply of oxygen for combustion. However, water is not a great idea for electrical fires as it may enable the fire to spread by conducting electricity throughout the area and potentially ignite other flammable materials. That's where BCF fire extinguishers come in. They are extremely effective for suppressing fires by using a chemical bonding process that disrupts the interaction of those three elements. It does not allow electrical conduction and is therefore safe when used around electrical appliances. It is also relatively non-toxic which, in a closed environment like an aircraft, has obvious advantages.

Sleepless in Seattle

Flying to the west coast of America carries with it a pretty severe time shift of minus eight hours compared to London. The early Seattle trip starts at home with a six in the morning alarm call, finally landing in Seattle thirteen and a half hours later. And the strange thing is that after a flight of 5000 miles and just under ten hours flying time, it always comes as a surprise when the friendly controllers say 'good morning' to you.

Arriving at the hotel feeling tired, there was little hope of sleeping because my adrenaline was still pumping and it was still only one o'clock in the afternoon there. Perhaps a couple of beers with the crew? Or a walk to the sea front, or a wander round the Pike Place indoor market area? I sometimes went there to watch the throngs of tourists stare reverentially at the first ever Starbucks, their selfie sticks capturing the moment for the folks back home. I used to stand with them, trying to pick up on the energy this shrine to caffeine was obviously generating, but I'm afraid to me, it was just a shop that sells coffee in paper cups. I just don't get it, but I'm sure I'm in the minority. I can see it doing really well for itself.

The Pike Place Fish Market is an entertaining place. Best known for the fishmongers who hurl customers' orders from one end of the stall to the other, where it is weighed and wrapped. No mean feat when they are tossing whole salmon weighing as much as five kilos. Sometimes, the staff startle the crowd by throwing an imitation foam fish into their midst. There is a sign above the stall that reads, 'Caution: Low Flying Fish'.

The rest of the large marketplace houses a jumble of artisan and curio shops of the kind popular at tourist spots. It rains a lot in Seattle, and sodden tourists traipsing through the covered alleyways and in and out of the shops, can unfortunately give the place the fuggy aroma of a wet dog on a public bus.

Victor Steinbrueck Park is close by. It is a pretty square of grass with sea views across Puget Sound and the quaint Bainbridge Island. It is also a favourite meeting place for the city's homeless. Seattle has the third largest number of homeless people in America and they are a tragic sight throughout much of the city.

Well-heeled citizens either simply ignore them or give them a wide berth as if complying with an invisible exclusion zone. The contrast between the affluent consumer-driven rich, and the filthy, lonely, broken homeless, is stark. Dispirited by this sad state of affairs, and by the eclectic aroma of fresh fish and over-hyped coffee,

I headed back to the hotel. I was knackered now and wanted to get some sleep. It was one in the morning body-time, but only five pm local. Unfortunately, there was someone next door who was very busy. Every five minutes he would open his bedroom door then let it swing closed with a full throttle slam. This went on for an hour. I guess it was entirely reasonable for him not to realise there was someone next door trying to sleep. But, bugger it. I got out of bed, picked up the kettle, and opened my door. I then bludgeoned the guy repeatedly over the head with the kettle before pushing him down the emergency stairwell.

Of course, I didn't do that, but if I could just get to sleep, I could have dreamed about doing it.

At four in the morning (now midday to me), I was awake and having breakfast in bed. I was amazed that the same door once again opened and closed with a teeth-rattling slam. Who has anywhere to go at four in the morning? Maybe he had his own bludgeoned corpse to dispose of? How bloody thoughtless can you be? Not the disposing bit, but the slamming bit.

It's Going to be a Bumpy Ride

Landing in windy conditions is always extremely challenging because the wind never behaves itself. On the approach to landing, gusting wind towards the aircraft has the effect of increasing airspeed and lift, necessitating a reduction of engine thrust and an increase in rate of descent to regain the correct approach profile. Insufficient distance to touchdown to apply corrective measures would require a go-around. Conversely, gusting winds from behind the aircraft robs speed and lift, causing the aircraft to sink. Engine power needs to be applied to regain both speed and height, and again if the losses are too extreme, a go-around would be required.

Crosswinds cause their own problems. If the aircraft is pointed at the runway with a strong wind from the side then obviously the aircraft would be blown off course. So, in order to track the aircraft along the extended line of the runway, the aeroplane is crabbed into the wind. The crab angle can be quite extreme in very strong crosswind conditions. The technique to landing in crosswinds is to maintain the crab angle until around thirty feet. The rudder (controlled by the feet) is then applied to swing the aircraft so that it now points down the runway. In doing this, one wing slices forward, picking up speed and lift and so rises. The other wing goes rearwards, loses lift, and drops, all resulting in an induced roll. The ailerons (the control surfaces on the wings) are used to apply an opposite roll to counteract this effect.

A split second later, the rate of descent must be reduced. Flaring the aircraft by gently pulling back on the control column ensures a smooth touchdown. All this is done using both feet and one hand. The other hand is used to control the engine thrust. Anyone sitting on the flight deck watching the pilot perform this task would see a coordinated cat's cradle of arms and legs all moving in opposite directions. Hopefully all the passengers feel is a beautifully smooth touchdown! If there is a go-around, then you know the pilot has run out of arms or legs, or both.

Once on the ground, the pilot uses both rudder and nosewheel steering to maintain the centreline of the runway whilst the gusty wind does its best to shuttlecock the aircraft in all directions. Before reverse thrust is applied, the pilot has a brief moment to decide whether the aircraft is in the correct position on the runway, that it is tracking down the centreline and hasn't landed too far down it. If the landing is unsatisfactory there is an option at this stage to apply full power and take the aircraft safety back into the air.

In September 2017, Hurricane Irma cut a swathe of destruction through the Caribbean before heading north to Florida. At times, it attained the highest strength category of any hurricane with peaked sustained winds of 180 mph. It claimed 134 lives and caused $77 billion worth of damage. On the 8th of September, its track took it just to the north of the Dominican Republic – coincidentally, on the same day I was due to fly there on a route check.

Our flight plan revealed that we would have to fly around the eye of the hurricane, and that our en-route and destination weathers would be at our operational limits. The flight would be extremely challenging, and I'm sure the examiner was very interested in our risk assessment and contingency planning for the day. It was my responsibility, as captain, to decide if the flight was safe to operate in the first place. If I didn't think it was safe, we wouldn't be going. In the early days of aviation there was a saying, 'there are old pilots and there are bold pilots but there are no old, bold pilots'. Thankfully that notion doesn't exist anymore. Our sole *modus operandi* is safety, followed by safety.

After careful consideration, we elected to take extra fuel to give us the option of diverting either to Saint Lucia, further south, or to the Bahamas, to the north-west. Both were forecast to be well clear of the effects of Irma. As it turned out, I didn't get the chance to put the plan into the action. The aircraft developed an engine technical issue that the engineers worked on for hours. In the end they decided the part could not be fixed, and it was replaced with a spare. Having re-boarded all the passengers and taxied out to the take-off position another similar but contradictory warning showed itself on the flight deck, requiring us to return to stand. It was a very frustrating day for everybody but by that time, we were pushing our maximum crew duty times and together with the challenging day ahead of us, I decided enough was enough. The passengers were taken to a hotel for the night and we all went home with the intention of trying again the next day.

The following morning, Irma had shuffled off to wreak havoc elsewhere, and we were looking forward to a relatively straightforward flight. As we were climbing out just south of Ireland, one of the crew rang to say a passenger in her seventies was having a suspected heart attack. I asked them to enquire if there was a doctor on board. In the meantime, we checked the weather for a diversion to Shannon, noted that the weight of the aircraft would need to be reduced by dumping fuel before we could land, and gave air traffic control a 'heads up' about what we might need to do.

Eventually the crew came back with an update on the passenger. It seemed the lady was travelling on her own, had started her journey in Rome, and didn't speak English. She had no credit cards with her and as she was not expecting to stay the night in the UK, she had no British currency. When she was taken to the hotel the previous evening, she hadn't understood that the company was providing not only accommodation, but also an evening meal and early morning breakfast before being taken back to the airport. The poor lady was a diabetic and hadn't eaten anything for the last fourteen hours! Honestly, our job involves trying to cover every possibility and eventuality but that one had slipped through the net. My heart bled for her. She soon recovered after some food and the crew took her under their wing and rather spoilt her for the rest of the flight.

The flight itself, after what it could have been the day before, was in all senses of the word, a breeze. Arriving at the resort, I was amazed how little damage it had suffered, but I'm sure that was due to the fact it had been built with hurricanes in mind. It was nice to unwind with the crew at the open-air bar. It was warm and calm and all seemed right with the world. Our revelries contrasted starkly with the experience of the previous crew, who were evacuated from the hotel and spent the night sleeping on the floor in a nearby sports hall.

Next day, I went for a walk on the beach which was self-advertised as one of the best beaches in the world. True, it was a long stretch of very fine, white sand dotted with palm trees. But it was also bloated with regimented rows of beach chairs that rather spoilt any idealised notion of a tropical paradise. And to seal the deal, a speaker the size of a small family saloon was thumping out aggressive dance music. The local sea birds loved it. The base was so powerful it was frightening the sand crabs out of their burrows, to be picked off by the eager gulls. It was crustacean carnage. I marvelled at a group of holidaymakers who had set up shop close to the speaker and were all dozing contentedly as if it was a quiet Sunday morning in a country garden. Perhaps they were deaf. If they weren't, they soon would be.

Another guest, sporting an impressively large belly came staggering towards me. Good for him, he was obviously enjoying the all-inclusive booze to the max. His small, black Speedo swimming trunks, still fashionable in certain countries, were inside out with the label flapping around his backside. I thought he was on his mobile phone but in fact he was slurring to himself with a Russian-esque accent. He tottered drunkenly towards the sea, wavered briefly and then collapsed face first towards the water. The only thing stopping him from sinking below the Plimsoll line was a mat of seething seaweed that had collected on the shore during the previous day's storm. As he hit it, thousands of sandflies erupted irritably into the air, buzzed around for a few seconds and then resettled on his corpse-like figure. He was fast asleep and, for all I knew, was being eaten alive. Still, they had a lot to go at.

A little further down the beach, a tanned and honed fitness instructor stood in front of a group of well-fed inmates. They were flailing around with uninhibited abandon to the beat of another equally large loud-speaker, which was competing with its sibling by hammering out a different base-heavy, dance track. Everyone seemed to be having a great time, but I found it all a bit too frantic and decided to retreat.

I was hoping for a quiet spot on the beach, in the shade, where I could read my book, but this was not the place for such tranquil pursuits. On the way back to my room, I spotted, some way out to sea, a very large metal cage. I later found out it was called Dolphin Island Park, a dolphin jail set permanently in the sea. It's very depressing to think these magnificent, intelligent creatures, perfectly evolved to roam the expanse of the oceans in large social communities, are still being imprisoned in these stark structures, purely for our entertainment. Surely we should find this sort of thing unacceptable now? If nobody visited or supported these places, they would soon close down. The Caribbean is beautiful and offers all things for all tastes, and the hotel guests appeared to be having a great time, but this resort wasn't for me.

Because the previous day's flights had been cancelled courtesy of Irma, our flight home was full to the brim. I even had cabin crew sitting on the flight deck for take-off in order to release their jump seats to get as many people home as possible. During the flight I had reports that a passenger in business class was having a tantrum. He was convinced another passenger was enjoying preferential treatment.

'He got his choice of salmon starter, why didn't I?'

'It's due to the fact that we are overbooked today, sir. I believe you were offered an alternative choice though?'

'Well, yes I was, but the fact remains that he got his first choice and I didn't.'

'Yes, sir. He was forcibly downgraded from first class as the flight is overbooked. Did you know his house has just been destroyed in the hurricane?'

'OK, but he still has his salmon starter, which is more than I've got.'

'Yes sir, he's obviously luckier than most.'

Double Dip

It was early December and I was visiting the 'Eisho-Jij' temple at Kamakura just outside Tokyo. It's not only beautiful but it also gives a real glimpse into traditional Japanese culture. As I drifted around the garden complex, I was feeling very otherworldly. Partly because it was so tranquil, so calm, just so 'right', but also because I was trying to shoehorn a plus nine-hour time change into my forty-eight-hour stopover.

It was important to try and adjust to local time as much as possible, not only so I could explore during their day, but also because the flight back started early morning Japanese time. It was essential I tried to have at least a semblance of a night's sleep before the journey home. With a flight time of just under thirteen hours and a seventeen-and-a-half-hour door to door day, it would be even more gruelling without some sleep beforehand.

So anyway, it was eleven o'clock in the morning in Japan, but two o'clock in the morning body time, and as my world shuddered slightly with circadian confusion, I was marvelling at the fanatical attention to detail that allows a Japanese garden to look so natural and jaw droppingly beautiful.

There is little left to chance. Everything had been placed with a specific aesthetic in mind. Even the space between things has a meaning in the Japanese garden, with the space carrying its own visceral purpose of highlighting the things around it. They call it *Ma*, and it's a fantastic way of looking at the world.

I stood and watched a gardener tend one of the thousands of *Niwaki* or cloud pruned pines. They are beautiful trees, shaped to look either ancient or wind-blown, or trained to provide a certain shadow, or reflections in the water. They require an extraordinary amount of attention. The specialist *Niwaki* gardeners, who undergo a seven-year apprenticeship, meticulously work on each tree for up to four days spread across the year. They tend every single inch of every single tree. And in typical Japanese fashion, my mood became pleasantly meditative as I watched this master work so calmly and methodically.

As I wandered further into the gardens, I passed many locals, most of whom were wearing white surgical masks, and I wondered why. (This was years before the world was hit with Coronavirus, and wearing a face mask, for a westerner, was as culturally odd as walking down your high street in a mankini.) I wondered if the locals were concerned about catching something, or were they wearing them out of consideration for other people, not wanting to spread their germs?

I looked into one of the courtyards and saw a man, perhaps in his eighties, stringing a bow and collecting half a dozen arrows. This simple task was done in such a thoughtful and measured way I couldn't help but be drawn in by the calmness of it all. He saw me watching and beckoned me closer. I had a very pleasant few minutes watching him concentrate solely on the task of notching an arrow, taking aim and loosing it at the target. Apart from the fact he was rather good, it was mindfulness at its best.

I left him to it after a while, acknowledging his invitation with a small nod of the head, which he returned with a bow. Nothing was said but everything communicated. I continued my journey through the temple complex, the sun on my back and a faint smell of wood smoke in the air. A young couple strolled towards me, clearly in love and at peace with the world, arm in arm in an affectionate embrace, her head rested gently on his shoulder. As they passed me, the man casually pulled down his white mask and sneezed into my face. So that answered my previous question then. He was totally indifferent, and it made me want to go and smash his face in, but instead I skulked off to the Zen garden to try and restore some balance to my mood. It was going to have to be a bloody good Zen garden.

It was there that I came across another important word used in understanding a Japanese garden: *Mu*.

The term *Mu* means emptiness. The idea of a Zen garden has fascinated me for years. On the face of it, the incredibly simple bed of white gravel has been raked with immaculate detail into waves, into which a small number of rocks are placed. The gravel represents waves in the sea and the rocks the island mountains of the eight immortals. *Ma*, the space between the waves, can be distilled into *Mu*, the pure emptiness which can still the mind and make it receptive to enlightenment. So that *Ma* becomes *Mu*.

Japanese gardens have been perfected over hundreds of years. Many of us in the west mistakenly assume they can be easily recreated back home. Just bung down some crushed slate, throw in a couple of acer trees, and a concrete cast of Buddha, and job done. And to a certain extent we have evolved the concept further than any Japanese gardener could possibly do. We have gone from *Ma* to *Mu* and now to *Me*. My meaning of *Me*, is:

Me (noun) short for mess, as in, 'what a bloody mess'.

Our hotel stands on the water's edge in a vibrant and upmarket area of Yokohama, some twenty miles south of Tokyo. Until 2012, the hotel was the tallest building in Japan, and whilst not in the same league as some of the world's tallest, seventy floors in one of the most active earthquake zones on the planet seems tall enough. It has seismic proof foundations, tuned mass dampers, and its floor to ceiling glass windows sit in substantial rubber isolators, all to mitigate the almost daily seismic events that shake the bejesus out of the city.

On one trip to Yokohama I had Pen with me. We used public transport to get about, crammed onto buses, trains and tubes with commuters, school children and elderly ladies with shopping trolleys. The Tokyo tube stations were a challenge; the signs were literally all in Japanese, but there was something magical about popping up from their crowded, frantic underground world to find ourselves in exquisite public gardens, or the tranquil grounds of Buddhist temples and Shinto shrines in and around Tokyo. (Buddhism was introduced into Japan in the sixth century CE. Shinto means 'the way of the gods' and is the indigenous faith, as old as Japan itself).

One evening on the way back up to our hotel room on the sixtieth floor, even the soothing music playing couldn't hide the fact that the lift had begun to shake alarmingly. It was only then that we realised why each lift in the hotel was furnished with two small chairs. Although in reality, I'm not sure how much help they would been in softening the blow as we plunged sixty floors at speed. With typical Japanese attention to detail, the hotel works. The air conditioning is efficient and silent, the curtains are black-out quality, and all the doors close softly and fit snugly, which prevents corridor noise from seeping inside the rooms. Whilst staying in Japanese hotels, there has never been the slightest impulse for me to bludgeon anyone with anything.

The ensuite bathrooms, unsurprisingly, have those Japanese techno-toilets. There have been many variations on a theme since the late 1800s, when Thomas Crapper patented his designs for what we now think of as the modern toilet. The French had a porcelain squatting hole in the floor, and the Germans, who are known for their heavy meat diet, have an elevated pre-water shelf so they can poke around looking for evidence of worms, or some such.

True to form, the Japanese have gone all technical. Their loos come with a control panel not dissimilar to those found on the flight deck, and one can call upon ablutionary services such as automatic lid opening and closing, seat heating, massage options and automatic flushing, along with gender specific adjustments for the water jet (front and rear), wash, wipe and blow dry.

Some even play music to 'relax the user's sphincter'. Apparently, some loos perform the first few phrases of Op. 62 Nr. 6 *Frühlingslied* by Felix Mendelssohn who, as you know, is famous for his sphincter relaxing compositions. Personally, that particular piece of music makes me want to buy a soft-serve ice cream from a mobile van rather than evacuate myself, but I guess there are cultural differences at work there. You can now buy talking toilets that greet the user, presumably with a chirpy, 'Hey, welcome bud, come sit down and take a load off', or the Japanese equivalent. More recent ideas include the addition of medical sensors that measure urine derived blood sugar levels, blood pressure, pulse and the body fat content of the user. The data can then be sent straight to a doctor through an internet connection. Presumably this feature doesn't come with FaceTime though.

The controls for my ensuite loo came with instructions both in Japanese and disturbing pictograms, and frankly I was scared to death of it. I was in constant fear of ending up with a camomile and lotus blossom power-enema followed by having my balls ripped off because I had incorrectly selected the wrong gender for the over enthusiastic wipe function. It always stayed powered down, in basic flush mode, but I knew it watched me, waiting for its chance.

The next morning it was home time. The wake-up call was 6:30 (21:30 UK time the previous evening, which is quite messed up isn't it.) I opened the curtains to a beautiful sunrise over Tokyo Bay.

The flight took us north with a fantastic view of Mount Fuji on our left. As we climbed, I realised the centre of the Chiba peninsula looks like a petrie dish full of dividing culture cells. They are in fact hundreds of golf courses, and each one is stunning. It's not only an area of outstanding natural beauty but it must also have the highest concentration of checked trousers and brightly coloured tank tops anywhere in the world. 1,700 miles into the flight, we passed just south of Yakutsk, Siberia, Russia, which has the honour of being the coldest city on earth, and that day it was an inhospitable minus 43°C. To the long-haul pilot though, it is a glorious oasis offering one of only a handful of diversionary airfields on this northerly route until European airspace some 2,700 miles later.

A quick glance at our outside air temperature showed it was -65°C. Aviation fuel freezes at about -45°C but is kept from doing so by a very clever system that uses fuel to cool the engine oil using a heat exchanger, returning the warmed fuel to the tanks.

An hour and a half later, we crossed the Arctic Circle* heading towards the Barents Sea. Being so far north, the sun was setting quickly and it was soon dark. As our latitude crested and we started to fly south, it wasn't long before the sun rose again to give us our second sunrise that day.

Because of delays in Tokyo and a particularly long flight time of well over thirteen hours, it was around 16:00 London time when we started our approach to land. The sun had started to set yet again, meaning I had seen two sunsets and two sunrises in a single day.

It was little wonder I spent most of my life not having a clue what day it was.

* The Arctic Circle is a line around the earth that marks both the northernmost point at which the centre of the midday sun is just visible on the winter solstice, and the southernmost point at which the centre of the midnight

sun is just visible on the summer solstice. Traveling further north from the Arctic Circle will give an increasing number of days of total daylight in summer and total darkness in winter.

One lump or two?

While we're on the subject of extreme chilliness, I never grew tired of spotting icebergs, often off the coast of Greenland. Some floated in solitary splendour, others gathered together in groups. When the sun caught them just right, these majestic behemoths glowed ice-blue, and they never failed to enthral me.

The iceberg that sank the Titanic in the early hours of Sunday 14th April 1912 most likely originated from the Ilulissat ice shelf on the west coast of Greenland. Today, radar, satellite photos, aircraft patrols and GPS have made the North Atlantic a much safer place for shipping. However, due to global warming it is estimated that there are far more icebergs floating around now than there were at the beginning of the twentieth century. The risk of a vessel striking an iceberg still remains.

Don't Know Whether to Laugh or Cry

I'm always struck by the unique atmosphere of an airport departure level. I'm sure you've noticed it too. It's basically a big cauldron of emotions, so strong they're almost palpable. It's like the opening montage in the Richard Curtis film 'Love Actually', but without the saccharine.

There are the sad travellers trying to be brave as they leave their loved ones. There are others on their way to reunite with the long lost, and almost bursting with anticipation. There are delayed passengers who are angry, tired or just beyond caring. There are stressed mothers coping with over-excited children. And, of course, you have the passengers who are petrified of dying. This emotional maelstrom of humanity is then crammed into a large tube and forced to coexist for hours. Their personal space is invaded from all directions, they are desiccated with altitude, fed crappy food, and thrown about in their turbulent seats.

The words spoken by the pilot over the PA system are designed to be an antidote to all these things. They hopefully convey that the chaps up front are professionals and that they will look after you. And they will. What they don't promise is that you are going to enjoy yourself. For most of us, air travel is no longer a luxurious, special event. How many times have you heard a pilot say, 'So sit back, relax and enjoy the flight'? It's well intentioned, but so inappropriate for today's mass market flights. It would be more honest to say, 'I hope the body odour of the

198

overweight chap sitting next to you isn't too overpowering. I hope you don't get deep vein thrombosis, or suffer from near-terminal flatulence from the rarefied atmosphere.'

Is it a Cloud or a Right Bastard?

It's not just the burgers that are supersized in America. Its weather can be pretty impressive too. I've written about the fun that can be had when operating there in winter. The summer months can be equally if not more challenging because the whole continent can suffer from regular thunderstorm activity the likes of which is rarely seen in the UK.

Lightning, heavy rain and occasionally hail, accompanied by ferocious turbulence, are the result of the broiling frenzy that is a cumulonimbus cloud. Their name is a bit of a mouthful; hence they are always referred to by their meteorological code name 'Cb', pronounced 'see-be'.

These towering beasts are produced through the convective uplifting of vast quantities of moisture laden air. They start near the ground or sea where warmed air expands, becomes less dense and rises. As the air rises to higher levels it begins to cool, and when cooled enough, like warm breath on a cold window, the water vapour condenses to form water droplets of cloud. This releases stored energy (called latent heat), making the air even more buoyant and it continues its climb skywards. Given the right conditions, like those seen in the hot humid summers typical in many parts of the world, these clouds can reach colossal proportions, and it's not uncommon to see them top out at forty or fifty thousand feet.

As the cloud matures, water droplets collide, combine, and become heavy enough to overcome the uplifting air, resulting in torrential rain which in turn creates equally sizeable down drafting air. The shearing effect of the upward and downward movement of this air leads to a frictional separation of electrical charge within the droplets. And when this has reached a large enough capacity, it discharges as lightning.

A typical Cb storm cloud (or cell) contains enough pent-up energy that, if it could be extracted, would be the equivalent to that produced by a nuclear power station operating at full chat for six months.

But that's just the mechanics of how they develop. To an observer on the ground, Cb clouds can look darkly menacing but, in general, you'll just get very wet. To an aircraft, however, they represent one of the villains in aviation mayhem, acting like Ivan the Terrible in a particularly bad mood. Some of these cloud cells contain turbulent shearing forces well in excess of the structural limits of the aircraft.

Within the storm cell, water droplets as cold as -40°C exist in a supercooled liquid state. Presented with something to freeze onto, for example an aircraft, this supercooled water would have a field day. It's been shown that ice can accumulate by up to one centimetre every minute on an aircraft flying through such clouds, and could easily swamp its de-icing capability.

In short, flying into a Cb is to be avoided.

All aircraft have an operational limit to how high they can fly. The 777, for example, has a ceiling of 43,000 feet. Avoiding these clouds by climbing over them is discouraged as they can develop so quickly as to out-climb the aircraft. In my experience the base of these clouds is rarely below 2,000 feet, and on final approach the aircraft is usually clear of the cloud itself. However, this presents one of the most hazardous times when operating in the vicinity of Cb activity. Sudden and torrential rain can lead to the loss of visual contact with the ground and the runway itself. This torrential rain can also cause the runway to flood, leading to a rapid and significant reduction in breaking ability.

Down drafts of turbulent air from Cb's can develop into a 'microburst' where intense columns of downward moving air exit the storm cell, hit the ground and spill out in all directions. This can cause significant and severe turbulence, and if the aircraft is on the downstream side of this out-flowing air, the wings can be robbed of lift, leading to a wing stall.

The weapons we bring to bear against such a formidable foe include weather radar systems; ground sensing microburst detectors and, more importantly, our knowledge of these weather systems, their behaviour and their effects. They are such an important phenomenon that we train, train, and train some more in order to avoid and if necessary mitigate their impact.

When in the cruise, we avoid individual cells by twenty-five miles. If cells collect as a storm front making it impossible to navigate through them, it's not unusual to have to deviate off the planned route by as much as two hundred miles.

Cb's are difficult to predict as they can develop, grow and subside in a matter of hours. So, whilst we know the conditions in which they will start to develop, it is very difficult to know where each individual storm cell will be at any given time. If one just happens to be in the vicinity of an airfield it can cause significant disruption as aircraft are routed around them.

They can be so troublesome that airports are forced to close entirely. And this is what we faced one day as we routed towards Houston, Texas. A long line of conjoined thunderstorms from Dallas to Houston became so severe that take-offs and landings were suspended at both airports.

Knowing there was a possibility of storm activity in the area we had taken substantial reserves of fuel - a decision we were now grateful for. Not being able to continue to Houston or indeed divert to Dallas, we backtracked our route and diverted to Atlanta, Georgia. A diversion of nearly six hundred miles and over two hours away, but it had the advantage of fine weather and was one of our regular scheduled destinations, which meant there was full operation support.

While we waited for conditions to improve in Houston, we refuelled, re-provisioned and re-flight planned. Crucially, we calculated the latest time we could depart Atlanta in order to make it to Houston and stay within our crew duty time limit. As captain, I had the power to extend the normal duty time limits by up to three hours, having first taken into account the fatigue levels of the crew and the expected conditions of flight.

The thunderstorms did eventually move away, and Houston reopened. Of course, things never quite work out as planned, and we were informed, whilst en-route, of further delays for arrivals into Houston due to the backlog of traffic trying to land there. Our given landing time meant we would exceed the absolute maximum duty time by twenty minutes, but what could we do? Houston was our closest airfield by then. In the end, our duty day was about eighteen hours, and whilst we were tired, we had the satisfaction of getting everyone safely to the right place.

The final arbiter on all safety related matters is the Civil Aviation Authority. Our case was referred to them for scrutiny. Using my report, which detailed the events of that day and my calculations on timings as well as reports from the airfields, it was concluded that my actions had been fairly judged and reasonable. I mention this just to point out that all our actions have to be accounted for to a higher, legal power.

Atlanta was our saviour on that occasion but it isn't always the good guy. A year later as we tried to make our approach there, we were once again working hard to avoid thunderstorms. Cumulonimbus clouds contain so much water that they appear as bright red returns on the weather radar, and there were so many of them we were constantly plotting and re-assessing our route through gaps between them.

The air traffic control environment at Atlanta, even at the best of times, is frantic. Add to this a sky full of storm clouds and the situation was becoming very, very busy with an increasing number of aeroplanes trying to use a smaller and smaller amount of viable airspace. We could see a large red storm return on the weather radar.

'Atlanta, we need a turn left or right thirty degrees. We have severe weather straight ahead.'

'Negative, you have traffic both sides of you.'

'How long before we can turn?'

'Less than a minute.'

'If we don't turn in thirty seconds we will be declaring an emergency.'

'Roger, stand by.'

I turned to Sam, the first officer: 'Sam, PA the cabin crew. Get them strapped in.'

ATC then cleared us to turn left onto a heading 240 degrees.

At that exact moment, another cell out to our right-hand side hit us with its best shot. There was an intensely bright flash, a loud bang, and I swear I felt the aircraft shake.

When I could see properly again, I quickly scanned the instruments to make sure the engines were still running, and that all the systems were normal. Much to my amazement, the aircraft didn't seem to have given a jot about the fact it had just been hit by lightning. We reported the strike to air traffic control, and engineers were ready to meet the aircraft on our arrival at the gate.

After a complete inspection of the aircraft, it turned out there were more than a hundred pockmarked holes running along its full length. The lightning bolt had hit the nose of the aircraft and then ricocheted in and out of the aeroplane as it made its way towards the back. You could see the exit mark underneath the tail section. The aircraft was grounded for over a week while repairs were carried out and it was certified fit for flight once again. It was the most severe lightning strike damage the engineer had ever seen. However, the aircraft did what it was designed to do, and allowed millions of volts of electricity to pass through it with little consequence to either its occupants or its systems.

Desperate Times

It's heartbreakingly sad that a combination of unimaginable desperation and a lack of understanding would drive someone to stowaway in the wheel well of an aircraft. Despite what the movies would have you think, it is not possible to access the inside of an aircraft from a wheel well. They are permanently unpressurised, and anyone hiding there would face a tragic raft of life-threatening obstacles. Immediately after take-off, the undercarriage is retracted inside the wheel wells, posing a serious risk of crushing injuries. As the aircraft gains altitude, pressure and temperature drop. Above approximately 10,000 feet declining oxygen levels would cause brain function to become increasingly impaired until eventually, and almost certainly, the individual would lapse into unconsciousness.

Although the outside air temperatures at cruising altitudes can be as low as -60°C, there would be an initial brief respite. The rate of temperature loss in the wheel well itself would be slowed by radiant heat from the undercarriage, brakes, hydraulic pipes and frictional heating of the aircraft skin. Eventually however this would dissipate and it would become extremely cold in the wheel well, perhaps -30°C. The stowaway's forced inactivity would almost certainly result in hypothermia, frostbite or simply freezing to death. Just as divers have to be careful not to surface too quickly or risk gas bubbles forming in their bloodstream, reduced pressure at altitude could cause decompression sickness leading to heart attacks and strokes.

If a person did miraculously manage to avoided brain damage, death from hypoxia or hypothermia, cardiac arrest or stroke as the aircraft descended, the air would warm and oxygen levels would increase. However, an unconscious or semi-conscious person would still be at risk of falling out of the wheel well once the undercarriage was lowered for landing. There have been instances of young, fit people stowing away and surviving, but the odds are incredibly slim. It almost always proves fatal. We are always extra vigilant at destinations where there is a high risk of stowaways. Before every flight one of the pilots carries out an inspection of the exterior of the aircraft and, in stowaway risk destinations, undercarriage spaces are inspected thoroughly. When taxiing out to the runway, extra care is taken to keep watch, and to minimise the time at the take-off holding position, where stationary aircraft provide an ideal opportunity for stowaways to gain access to the wheel wells.

Mumbai in India has a typically no-nonsense approach to guarding against stowaways whilst taxing out. Guards are placed at regular intervals around the runway to keep watch. Their other task is to scare birds from the take-off path by firing shotgun blanks. It's possible that a potential stowaway would think they are live rounds, and be deterred.

Taxiing out for take-off at Mumbai airport was always an uncomfortable experience for me. Only a hundred meters away from the take-off position and flowing just outside the perimeter fencing, is a fetid, stinking and highly polluted river. Alongside the river sits a huge shanty town of makeshift dwellings beneath blue tarpaulin covers. It houses some of the city's poorest people and I've seen it in stifling heat and humidity, and awash with monsoon rains. Either way, it must be a grim existence for its inhabitants.

The slum's residents would often watch us as we taxied past. We were affluent Westerners sitting in air-conditioned comfort, in our crisp, short sleeved, white shirts, having just had a nice cup of tea. And I suspect we were all looking at each other and thinking, 'what must it be like to be there?' And I thank God for my good fortune.

On one particular flight from Mumbai, we were given take-off clearance but delayed slightly to interrogate the weather radar. There were a lot of shower clouds ahead and we would need to pick our way around them. Once airborne, we raised the landing gear and moments later we heard loud and constant banging from under our seats.

I followed the standard operating procedure by engaging the autopilot and handed over control of the aircraft to the first officer. This allows the captain to monitor and manage the overall situation without being burdened with the actual flying of the aircraft. We didn't know what was causing the banging and therefore we went through all the various possibilities, using our always useful TDODAR diagnostic tool to help us. Right away the T for time came to the fore. We needed to create time to allow us to diagnose the issue, and telling ATC immediately got us the help we needed. The excellent controller gave us vectors away from other traffic and the ever present weather.

Did we have a stowaway in the nose-gear wheel well? It was foremost on our minds, and the banging was coming from exactly the right spot.

Was there someone in the avionics bay? It sits just beneath our seats and houses radio, navigational and flight control computers. It is possible to access to it for ground maintenance and there was a slim chance we had unknowingly departed with someone still in there.

Finally, there was a third option. Was there a loose panel on the outside of the aircraft?

There was very little we could do to test the first two options, so we tested the third theory. Increasing our airspeed gave a marked increase in the level and rate of banging, accompanied by significant vibration throughout the aircraft. Slowing down again reduced the levels to a manageable state. We therefore discounted the possibility that we were carrying either an unwilling, disgruntled engineer, or a stowaway, and concluded there must be a loose panel.

The obvious danger here was that the panel would detach itself and be ingested by one of the engines, or that it hit and damaged one of the flight control surfaces. We therefore slowed right down and informed air traffic control that we would need to return to Mumbai. Before doing that, we would also need to jettison forty tons of fuel in order to reduce to our maximum landing weight. This would be achieved by pumping fuel from the tanks to special nozzles located near each wingtip.

The excellent Indian air traffic controller allotted us airspace that would keep us over the sea and away from the high mountains inland, allowing us sufficient space to manoeuvre around the developing storm clouds and to remain high enough for us to jettison our fuel. If conditions allow, for ecological reasons, it is recommended to jettison fuel at an altitude of at least 6,000 feet. This allows the fuel to completely vaporise before reaching ground level. It always pained me to have to jettison fuel like this. It is such a waste, and to give you an idea, this jettisoned fuel would have heated my home for the next 20 years!

We planned for all the possibilities we could think of: The undercarriage might not lower correctly, and if it didn't, how each failed landing gear would affect the landing. How would we handle a go around if that became necessary? Were we using the most suitable runway? Were the emergency services on standby and where were they positioned? (There are procedures for all these eventualities and they are part of our simulator training.)

Having spoken to the passengers we then briefed the cabin crew that the most likely outcome would be a safe and normal landing, but to be aware that should the aircraft veer off the runway, an evacuation might be necessary. Of course, the landing went smoothly and, on the ground, we parked up and met with the ground engineer. One of the actuator arms which closes the left nose-gear door had sheared, leaving the six-foot-long door flapping in the airstream. We wouldn't be going anywhere that day, so all the passengers were offloaded and taken to overnight accommodation.

It was obvious the aircraft would be out of action for a while and so arrangements were made to put the passengers and cabin crew on the next available flight to London, leaving us three pilots to wait for the aircraft to be mended. As it happened, there were no spares available in the whole of India so a part was requested from London.

India is infamous for its bureaucratic processes, and it has been said that if something is simple then Indian bureaucracy will complicate it. As an example, when entering or leaving the country the aircraft captain is required to sign up to ten different documents relating to the flight and its crew. Many of these signatures are made in huge, immaculately bound leather ledgers. Goodness knows where they are all kept but it must be a very large building. The process is smoothed by a chaperone who typically leads the procession of crew through the various checkpoints and officials, pointing to where a signature is required. I'm sure over the years I have probably unwittingly signed away the deeds to my house or committed my children to serve in their armed forces or something.

So it was in typical Indian fashion that when the spare parts arrived from London, they were delayed in customs for twenty-four hours before being released to the engineers. Sadly, London had sent a right-hand door and actuator rather than the left, so the whole process had to be repeated, taking another forty-eight hours for the parts to be delivered to the engineer. When he eventually received them, he fixed the problem within a couple of hours!

We whiled away our extended stay by eating truly excellent curries, seeing the sights of Mumbai and enjoying some retail therapy. I love shopping in India. Wherever you go, the shopkeepers are so keen to make a sale they will tell you the most outlandishly incorrect rubbish you could possibly imagine. As I approached the vast indoor market, I was intercepted by a gentleman who proclaimed, 'Sir, I know exactly the right stall for you to get your shopping'.

'But I haven't said what I was looking for.'

'OK, what do you want?'

'A king sized water bed, with a gentle wave function,' I ribbed.

He didn't miss a beat. 'Yes of course we can get you that, but what else are you looking for?'

I liked this chap immensely. 'I'm looking for a dark burgundy-red rug.' It was for the living room at home.

'I know exactly the right carpet for you. Please come this way.'

'OK, but just to be clear, I don't want any pashminas or fake handbags.'

I spent the next ten minutes trailing after him through the labyrinth of the market until we eventually arrived at what was probably his family's stall. He proudly laid out a carpet in front of me.

'It really is a very nice carpet,' I said, 'but as you can see, it's blue.'

'Well, it has shades of red.'

I raised my eyebrows at him. There were no other colours in the carpet but blue.

'So, perhaps for another room then,' he said with a cheeky smile.

For the next few minutes, I was shown all the pashminas and handbags I had already explained I didn't want, before we moved on to cushion covers. Having finally exhausted the possibility of a pre-sale, he brought out a carpet that was pretty perfect. We haggled over the price, and he said he would throw in the blue carpet for a special price. It wasn't so special, as it was two carpets for the price of two. We agreed on the price for the one carpet. I still have it in our living room at home and it always brings a smile to my face.

Do You Have What it Takes?

There are stereotypical images everywhere. And I suppose they have been formed, in some measure, out of partial truths. But just as *all* French men don't wear stripey shirts and berets and travel around on onion laden bicycles, we Brits don't all eat roast beef and pick fights at football matches.

And if there is a stereotypical image of an airline pilot, it was probably formed way back in the 1960s. Most airline pilots from that period were male and predominantly ex-military, where medical entry requirements demanded at least 20x20 vision and a medical record so perfect that even a family history of hay-fever would be a disqualifying factor. In short, they were in the peak of health. They were also self-assured, self-sufficient and with a slight propensity for rule breaking and aggression. Literally gung-ho and maverick. We are a more diverse bunch now with an increasingly large number of female and LGBTQ+ crew.

In general, we are task focused, thrive in challenging situations, have good hand-eye coordination and the ability to carry out fast and accurate computational analysis, plus the ability keep calm in often very stressful situations.

However, along with these similarities, we exhibit different and wide-ranging characteristics. I for one am a 'pragmatist' character type. I'm not that interested in the minutiae of how things work. Having said that, I have a detailed working knowledge of how the aircraft systems function and how they integrate into the whole. If things go wrong, I know how to deal with the failure, and operate the aircraft safely. I'll definitely even get a buzz about the extra challenge it creates.

But I don't really care how a particular piece of equipment failed or the mechanics of mending it... because I can't mend it. So, if I'm flying with a 'theorist', I can find it wearisome. They are the steam engine enthusiasts, who have to know how every nut and bolt fits together and with what torque setting. There is nothing wrong with that - they are incredibly knowledgeable people, but it's just not me.

I don't particularly enjoy listening to someone talk enthusiastically about electro-mechanical isolation valves and the role they play in making a *dubry ferkin* work properly. Luckily for me these characters are few and far between, and on the whole the flight deck is a very pleasant and relaxed place to spend the day with like-minded souls.

The cabin crew joke that the difference between God and an airline pilot is that God doesn't think he's a pilot. Funny, but a little harsh.

Years ago, I remember watching a programme featuring an American airline. The interviewer was on the flight deck talking to the captain, who was relaxed, good humoured and clearly loving his job. He was asked to name the most important characteristic of a successful airline pilot.

He thought for quite a while, surveying the hundreds of instruments on the flight deck, the cobalt blue sky, and the vast and beautiful world drifting slowly by beneath him.

Finally, he said, 'Well, if I've got to name one thing, I'd say, you've got to like chicken'.

Clearly, he didn't have an ego to maintain and actually, I think that's true for most airline pilots.

And all I can say is, no matter how much that captain liked chicken, if he had ever flown with a flight engineer, he wouldn't have got a look in.

Just occasionally, there are pilots who are on the very edge of what would be considered socially normal. During a quieter part of a flight to Chicago (our longest route with just two pilots) I was about to ask Peter, the first officer, a question about his life to kick-off a conversational exchange, but he buried his head in the newspaper. No problem, I thought, he probably just wants a bit of peace and quiet. But after a few seconds he made a 'tsk' sound, and proceeded to read aloud the entire article he deemed tsk-worthy. He then offered a black and white opinion on the piece that bordered on a fanatical rant.

Obviously a man of high spirit and passion. Maybe he was part Italian. It was clear my thoughts were not required because he buried his head in the paper again in order to reload for the next bombastic rant. Now, I like to natter as much as the next man, and I am genuinely interested in other people's lives, but if it's not a two-way conversation, then it is literally not a conversation.

Eventually the newspaper topics were exhausted, and he moved on to the controversial and highly risky subject of education. He asked how I had educated my children, giving me a glimmer of hope that, despite the subject matter, I might be allowed to contribute to the conversation. But I didn't get a chance to answer.

Instead, he set off with a detailed monologue of his thoughts on the schooling system, including university fees, then moved on to the health service, politics and the state of our roads. Having exhausted these subjects, he went on to tell me how well he was doing. The car he drove, the house he had just bought and his plans for it. Apparently, he was going to install all the modern domestic cliches: a wet room, roll top bath, an Aga, a Norwegian stove and a polished concrete floor, probably all in the same room for all I could tell, or cared.

I started out being socially polite. I nodded in all the right places and smiled at all the right moments, until my face muscles started to cramp and I had to stop. Eventually I ended up looking at him like some sort of vacant zombie. He didn't notice; he was in full flood and having a whale of a time. I wished I was. The occasional time I tried to join in, I was either ignored or contradicted. I started playing a game whereby I effectively repeated what he had just said, and then waited for him to disagree with it. Suddenly, I had a flash of inspiration. I picked up my iPad and began to study it in great detail, assuming he would pick up on the social cues and body language, and leave me alone. But he didn't.

I realised I was facing the next seven hours literally strapped into my seat in a space the size of a broom cupboard whilst he pontificated me to death. I was beginning to panic and, in the end, I said the most stingingly rude thing I think I've ever said to anybody in my life:

'Well, you are obviously really very pleased with yourself.'

And you know what? It didn't even register.

My despairing outburst reminds me of a two-way conversation I overheard between controllers in India some years back. We were flying over the Indian Ocean, well out of normal radio range, and in the days before satellite communications, we were using the High Frequency (HF) radio instead. Normal radio communications such as cell phone, TV and radio are all in the UHF and VHF frequency bands, and are roughly 'line of sight', that is, there has to be an uninterrupted straight-line path between sender and receiver. Obviously, the higher you are, the further you can see and the greater the line-of-sight distance.

There is a formula for calculating this distance depending on how high the sender/receiver is. I won't bore you with the formula, but basically it means if you stood on a beach at sea level, the horizon, and therefore the line of sight, is about three miles away. You would be able to see and talk via radio to a person sitting in a boat at that distance. Any further and they would have disappeared over the horizon. (Except of course if you belong to the flat earth society when your radio would presumably work for many thousands of miles.)

At cruise altitudes, say 35,000 feet, the line-of-sight distance is around 240 miles. Any further from a land-based radio, there is silence. To get over this issue, HF (high frequency) radios are employed. The properties of radio waves in this frequency range means they are reflected off the ionosphere, and communications can literally bounce around the world. Using ionised air to reflect radio means it's not the clearest of signals and because of its ultra-long range, the same frequencies used around the globe can interfere with each other. And it's with this last fact in mind, that I finally get around to the point of this tale.

For some ridiculous reason known only to the majesty of Indian bureaucracy, both Delhi and Bombay (still known as Bombay then) were using the same HF frequencies, and every man and his dog passing through both areas, transiting the Middle East, Far East and Indian Ocean were all trying to get a word in edgeways.

All the aircraft and the controllers in both Delhi and Bombay regions were stepping on each other's calls, and if it hadn't been important that they made themselves heard, it would have been comical.

Finally, out of the blue we heard the Delhi controller say:

'Bombay, Bombay this is the Delhi controller. Shut up.'

'Delhi, this is Bombay, no you damn well shut up.'

Delhi: 'Shut up, just shut up for a minute.'

Bombay: 'Fine, get on with it.'

There was a deafening silence as everyone waited to hear what would happen next, and in the brief pause I managed to make my radio call, pretending I'd just come onto the frequency. Was honesty the best policy between the two controllers? Not really. It all degenerated into chaos again within a matter of minutes. Then with typical antipodean directness, an Aussie pilot said: 'change your bloody frequencies mate'.

And I guess after the relevant forms were filled out in triplicate, signed and counter signed by the relevant authority, they probably were.

A Friendly Island

The distance from London to Barbados is 3,500 miles, with a flying time of eight and a half hours. Having crossed Land's End, there is nothing but sea until you get there. And what a thrill it is to see the emerald green land edged with white sand beaches and silver surf, slowly reveal itself. I still marvel at the technological advances of the twentieth century. Less than a lifetime ago, long distance air travel was navigated using a sextant! When I first started flying with the airline thirty years ago, I flew with captains who had actually used astronavigation to cross the Atlantic. We now take it as read that, after all that time in the air, the aeroplane will pop out of cloud with not just the island but also the runway in front of us.

Much has been written on the subject of 'place lag', and it is no more startlingly illustrated than setting off on a cold, rainy, winter's morning in the UK to arrive, an office day later, in a subtropical paradise. From the grey gloom of London to the startlingly vivid blues, greens and whites that promise warm seas, sun, and cooling drinks. The aircraft doors open and the air hits you with the hair-dryer heat of the trade winds. It can be literally dizzying, as your travel-tired body tries to assimilate this sensory assault.

I love the crew hotel in Barbados. We have been in residence for at least fifteen years, and that's very unusual. Quite often we are kicked out of a hotel after a period of time either because the hotel starts to charge the company too much, or they simply get fed up of us. Embarrassingly the last time I arrived in Antigua, I was met by the hotel manager who requested I ask the crew not to enjoy themselves quite so much as they were, frankly, pissing off the other guests. Shortly after this, the company were asked to find somewhere else to stay. We ended up being sent back to the Hotel Infectious Grande. Luckily by then I had the seniority to avoid the dump. Anyway, whatever the reason for our longevity in Barbados, it's a great place for a stop-over. It speaks volumes to us temperate dwellers that the reception and public areas are open to the elements and the cooling ever-present trade wind breeze. Why not, when the temperature never drops below about 23°C?

One of our first officers is part Barbadian and he often speaks of the importance of adjusting to Barbados time. He isn't talking about the time on the clock, but the pace of life. It's wonderfully laid back. Once, my son and I were a little late for our diving trip and were walking towards the dive shop at a brisk UK pace. It was clearly an astonishing sight for the locals because one stopped his car, wound down the window and, with genuine concern in his voice, shouted, 'Slow down or you'll have a heart attack'.

On another occasion, the dive leader was giving a brief to a load of newbies, and offered this useful advice: 'As you get into the water, there is no rush. As you descend the rope, there is no rush and as you swim along, there is no rush. Basically... there is no rush.' One of the nervous novices asked if there was anything in particular he should watch out for, and the dive leader replied, 'Yes, just remember to breathe'.

When asked to show my dive credentials, I give them a small booklet containing my photo and qualification certificates. Without exception, they open the front page, do a double take, and then crease up with howls of laughter. I get the same reaction pretty much everywhere in the world when I go diving. Some even manage to splutter something along the lines of it not being proof of my diving prowess but more of a relic from pre-history.

I learnt to dive at the age of twelve, which in those days was the earliest age deemed suitable for young lungs to experience pressurised air. By the time I was sixteen, I had started my own diving club with an ex-police diver. My dive book still has the original black-and-white photograph taken when I was about fourteen. It was the mid-1970s, and I had long, uncontrollable hair, was wearing a hideous shirt with large penny round collars, and sporting a deep tan from two weeks in the latest European 'bloody dump' my parents had taken us to.

One of the best perks of the job was taking my family with me on trips during the school holidays. Both my kids learnt to dive as teenagers and, because diving in Barbados is perfect, it became a popular destination for us. The dive shop is only four minutes by flip-flop from the hotel and some of the best diving in the area is in Carlisle Bay, a marine park, about four minutes by boat. The bay has six wrecks that can be easily explored in a fifty-minute dive.

Forgive me for going slightly off topic here, but each wreck has such a different story I hope you'll think it worthwhile. One of my favourite wrecks is the 'Bajan Queen'. Originally it started life as a tugboat called the Pelican but was subsequently renamed and converted into a party boat. By 2002 it had reached the end of its working life, presumably because it was riddled with rust as a result of all the spilt booze and vomit. It was probably quite deaf too. Deliberately sunk in Carlisle Bay, it sits upright on the sea bed, looking genuinely at peace with itself. It now provides pleasure in a very different way to scores of calm, quiet divers. I started diving on it in 2005 and it's been a pleasure to watch the sea life colonise it over the years. You can enter the wreck and swim through the engine room, complete with its two large diesel engines, then into a lower anti-room and from there up a spiral staircase onto the bridge, and then out again.

In 1990, the 'Eillion' came to Barbados from Columbia. When the ship was seized by local authorities and searched, they found the entire vessel was lined with marijuana. The government took control of the ship, and after all the legal issues were taken care of, it was taken out into the bay, and sunk. The way it sits on the seabed allows a small airlock to form in the bow of the ship, with each visiting diver contributing a little of their own air supply to maintain it. Both my children and I have used the airlock to have brief and quite surreal conversations twenty-five feet below the sea surface. It is also possible to swim through the superstructure in the stern of the ship but having been snagged on protruding pieces of metal several times in very confined spaces, I don't find it that enjoyable.

The story goes that, during World War One, the crew of the French tugboat 'Berwyn' sought shelter in the bay after being fired upon in battle. They were so enamoured by the hospitality of the locals and their rum, they asked the captain if they could stay a while longer. He replied 'over my dead body and a sunken ship'. After a few more barrels of hospitality the crew decided to take the captain up on his offer. They sat out the rest of the war by opening up the sea vents and letting the boat sink.

It is perhaps not widely known that, during the Second World War, the Caribbean was involved in a naval campaign waged by German and Italian submarines in an attempt to disrupt Allied supplies of oil and other materials. In 1942, the Canadian National Steamship 'Cornwallis' was harboured in Carlisle Bay, protected by anti-torpedo netting stretched across the bay from Needhams Point to Pelican Island. On September 11th, German U-Boat U-514 fired a total of six torpedoes into the bay, over a fairly leisurely thirty-minute period.

The Master of the 'Cornwallis', Captain Duncan MacLeod, on hearing the first torpedo explosion on the harbour defences, ordered the anchor raised and the main engines started. Unfortunately, it wasn't enough to save the steamship from attack. The initial volley significantly damaged the anti-torpedo netting, allowing the sixth and final torpedo to hit the 'Cornwallis' and blow a hole in her side some forty-four feet long and fourteen feet deep.

In spite of this, the captain managed to beach the ship and prevent it sinking. It was eventually repaired and returned to service in August 1943. In a sickening reminder of how vulnerable Atlantic shipping was during this period, sixteen months later it was torpedoed again in the Gulf of Maine. The Master, thirty-five crew members and seven gunners were lost. There were only five survivors.

During the Carlisle Bay attack in 1942, showing true heroism and real Dads' Army Britishness, four men took a small motorboat, armed with two depth charges strapped to the stern, out to where they thought the submarine might be. Having never used a depth charge before and unsure if they themselves would be damaged when it detonated, they nevertheless guessed a setting of six hundred feet and dropped it into the water. It didn't detonate, presumably because the sea bed wasn't deep enough, and as far as anyone knows it's still out there. After the attack, eyewitnesses reported seeing the U-boat surface, hoist a sail on the conning tower to give it the appearance of a small fishing boat, and simply sail away.

The section of the 'Cornwallis' bulkhead blasted off by the torpedo is now home to the most magnificent array of marine wildlife you could hope to see so close to shore.

One of the dive leaders is a lovely Bajan chap called G. I'm not protecting his name here; he introduces himself and is known simply as G. He sports the coolest dreadlocks I've ever seen, is unfailingly cheerful, positive and endlessly patient with nervous novices. He announces his arrival on the dive boat by blowing into his conch shell and saying, 'I love this thing, I call her Me-shell'.

One time, my daughter and I came across him whilst on a dive. We were thirty feet down and he was running across the sea floor at some speed. He was wearing his board shorts, a mask, and breathing from the air tank resting on his shoulder as if he was carrying a small log. He noticed us, stopped and waved as though we were passing in the street, and then off he went into the haze, like one of the undead characters in 'Pirates of the Caribbean'.

The beach at the hotel is beautiful. In one corner there is Fort Charles, built in 1650 as part of the British defences, and it retains its original plan. Three sides of the fort dip their toes into the sea and, amazingly, at the base of the south facing wall, twenty or more old cannons have been thrown into the sea to protect the fort from the relentlessly pounding waves.

There are no private beaches on Barbados and although some distance from the main hotel hubs, it still gets its share of beach hawkers. One lovely gentleman has a great sales pitch and I'm sure he would do really well on 'The Apprentice':

'Hi I'm Michael. Would you be interested in a massage today? Just so you know, I'm no homo and no pervert.'

I can't end this section without mentioning a beachside shack called 'Cuzz's'. To look at it you might assume that if you went within ten yards of it, you would risk an immediate and catastrophic health issue. In reality, Cuzz serves the finest, tastiest fish burger you could wish for, and I, along with thousands of others, can highly recommend it.

Out Of Their Comfort Zone

If you are a frequent flyer, you might be surprised to learn that in 2016 a UK national newspaper claimed nearly a quarter of all Britons had never flown. Ever. In 2017, the CEO of Boeing thought that around eighty percent of the world's population had never taken a single flight. And out of those that *have* flown, a proportion would approach the prospect with the same enthusiasm as they would a root canal filling. He didn't say that bit. I did. So, whilst flying has become almost an every-day event for some, it is a totally alien world for others, with its accepted conventions as baffling as many Americans' views on gun control.

There are first-time travellers from socio-economic groups with no exposure to modern jet transportation, who are therefore confronted with an unnatural and confusing situation. They are making a quantum leap away from their normal lives, so it is entirely understandable they revert to what they know, making mistakes and sometimes a mess, along the way.

During my days on TriStar, when security wasn't as thorough as it is now, there was a report of an unpleasant smell in the cabin several hours into the flight. The source of the smell was narrowed down when one of the passengers complained of being dripped on by a smelly, cloudy liquid. When the cabin crew investigated the overhead locker, they found a very large, long dead and over ripe catfish, wrapped in paper. It had started to ferment and bloat due to the reduced cabin pressure and there was a real risk it would explode, spreading its aromatic joy to everyone.

The passengers who had put it in the overhead locker couldn't understand what all the fuss was about. They often gave this local delicacy as a gift to their hosts. Although they admitted the hosts were normally only in the next village and not an eight-hour flight away. And if they had realised the cabin crew would be pushing a small, metal, gift-laden shop on wheels through the aeroplane, they would not have bothered with the fish. About a year later, on a similar route with the aircraft completely full, the cabin crew were working hard to ensure everyone's luggage was safely stowed before the flight departed. A lady sitting in an aisle seat was trying to breastfeed her baby as inconspicuously as possible considering she was surrounded by three hundred other passengers, all of whom were trying to settle into their own seats. She had a huge bag of baby essentials on her lap which was doubling up as a privacy screen. A cabin crew member walked by, pointed to it, and said, 'I'm sorry, but as soon as you can, that will have to go into the overhead locker'.

Before take-off the crew member went back down to give the mother an extension seatbelt. (These are used to secure babies to an adult's seatbelt during take-off and landing.) 'Madam, where is your baby?' she asked.

The lady looked up. 'Where you said he had to be.'

On further investigation, the baby was found fast asleep in a makeshift cot of jumpers and coats in the overhead locker.

Several times each year we find evidence that the modern, vacuum flush, aeroplane toilet is not as obvious a piece of equipment as you might think. The toilet floor will sometimes be flooded with water. No, not a fire-hose male traveller who is incapable of aiming properly, but someone who has never had access to, or used, toilet tissue. Instead, they resort to familiar habits and wash themselves down with water. And, just occasionally, the toilet itself will also bear no resemblance to their facilities at home. Presumably causing total confusion, it will have been ignored and instead a pile of poo will be found nestling on the floor in the corner of the lavatory cubical.

And then there are the passengers who, on hearing the 'twenty minutes to landing' information call to the cabin crew, instead of sitting down and buckling up, will actually get out of their seats, gather their things, and trundle them to the aircraft door where they will stand patiently as if on the number thirty-nine bus approaching their stop.

I was reading the 'Times of India' in Delhi recently about a village community thrown into confusion when a ten kilogram chunk of ice landed in a field nearby. They heard the thump as it hit the ground and went to investigate. They described what they found as, 'a stone that was ice cold with a transparent surface'. Some thought it was a meteorological phenomenon, others extra-terrestrial.

Several quick-thinking villagers chipped samples off it and stored them in their fridges so that 'experts' would be able to analyse them. In a marvellous piece of understatement, it was reported that after the investigation, residents were 'disappointed' to discover the item was not a meteorite. The gift from the sky was determined to be blue ice, a mixture of chemicals and human excrement that had leaked from the collection tank of an aircraft's toilets.

Lost in Translation

It's sometimes hard to get your point across. I'm sure many of you have played the game where a phrase is whispered into your neighbour's ear and the message is then relayed around the room in a similar fashion until the last person says what they heard. So that, 'it's a lovely day for a walk' is misheard and misinterpreted so many times it somehow becomes, 'Jack, I hate your guts and I want a divorce'.

The most famous example was a wartime request: 'Send reinforcements, we are going to advance.'

The tale goes that by the time the message reached HQ, it had become: 'Send three and fourpence. We are going to a dance.'

A phrase doesn't have to be repeated multiple times before its meaning is changed. Consider the phrase: 'Let's eat, dad.' By removing the comma after the word 'eat' you turn a hungry child into a hungry cannibal.

Then there are words that sound the same but have different meaning, for example two, to, or too, and deciding which witch is which can be difficult. (And how many of you didn't see the word 'witch' just now?)

Why am I wittering on about this? Well, pilots operate in a technically sophisticated environment. It's quite noisy and all communication is done through headset and microphone, often talking to people whose first language is not English. Even talking between ourselves has its own difficulties. We are strapped into our seats facing forwards and partly isolated with noise cancelling headsets, often missing the subtleties of body language that is so important for effective communication.

You'll be pleased, and possibly not surprised by now, to learn that a great deal of thought has gone into the art of aviation communication. There are rigid rules in place to avoid any risk of a misunderstanding. For example, when we fly at altitude we use the term Flight Level, where flight level eight zero (FL80) equates roughly to 8,000 feet. Air traffic control would never instruct an aircraft to 'climb to eight zero' because the 'to' could be misinterpreted as 'two', making the instruction sound like 'two eight zero'. Flight Level two eight zero (FL280) is roughly 28,000 feet, somewhat more than the intended eight thousand. And going there without clearance from ATC could very well spoil the day for a lot of people.

The word 'to' is never used when it could be misinterpreted as the number two. So, 'climb Flight Level eight zero' is the correct way to give this instruction. The word 'to' is missed out and the qualifiers 'climb' and 'flight level' are used to indicate the instruction relates to elevation.

When giving an instruction to turn onto a heading, it is always qualified to distinguish it from an elevation instruction. So, the instruction, 'turn left heading zero eight zero (080) degrees' indicates a direction and not an elevation. All instructions from air traffic control are required to be repeated back, word for word, by the pilot, as a check they have been heard correctly. On the subject of hearing, it is the first sense that is ignored by the brain when it's really busy. We've all experienced it. You're engrossed in reading or writing an email and your partner says something to you. Your brain prioritises your busy thoughts over hearing, and discards what your partner said. You might manage an affirmative 'mmm', but in fact you have no idea what they were talking about. Leading to the familiar, 'you never listen to a word I say to you'. Which you probably didn't hear either.

Combined with the fact that the short-term memory (anything the brain processes in the last thirty seconds) can only hold around seven bits of information, you can see why the feeding of verbal information in the correct way is vitally important.

Good air traffic controllers will break up a lengthy instruction into bite sized chunks. They know that in a busy flight deck environment, pilots will be using up a substantial amount of their brains' short-term memory resources, so they drip feed information to the pilots at a rate they can absorb it. UK controllers are superb at this; others aren't so good.

I remember listening to an American controller who, unlike his colleagues, misguidedly thought it was an indication of his own ability that he could rattle out instructions at the same speed as one of those financial services adverts - the ones that talk about APR and end breathlessly with, 'terms and conditions apply and always read the label before the best by date', or some such. One of the American pilots replied to him, very slowly: 'Sir, this is the rate at which I speak, and it is also the rate at which

I can listen, so if you want me to do something, you're gonna have to say it all again, but slower.'

It was a testament to the controller's narcissistic and flawed opinion of himself that he decided it was the pilot who was at fault. He repeated his instruction in such a slow patronising way he could have been talking to a four-year-old on the naughty step.

I waited for our turn to be machine-gunned down with his blistering tsunami of words, but I'd armed myself with a pen and paper so I didn't miss anything. I wasn't going to give him the pleasure.

If you wanted to clarify what someone had said to you, you would ask them a question, wouldn't you? And the majority of those questions would be 'closed questions', wouldn't they? Both of the above questions are easy to ask and even easier to answer, but closed questions can have serious shortcomings in aviation.

'He said climb flight level 280, didn't he?' is a closed question.

Firstly, it's a leading statement that suggests a 'yes' answer is required whether or not it is the correct answer. Firing back a 'yes' is simple, easy and requires no thought whatsoever from the person being asked the question. It closes down the conversation, but it has neither confirmed the understanding of the original instruction nor allowed for any subsequent questions.

Asking 'open questions' is much more effective, and it is a technique we use a lot on the flight deck.

'What level do you think we are cleared to?' is the 'open' way of asking the same question. It requires an understanding and cognition of the question in the first place and more than a yes/no answer as a reply. If the reply you get back is FL280 and you were thinking FL80 then you know that one of you heard it incorrectly and it needs to be clarified.

I was chatting to a Swedish first officer on our way to Bangkok. He said that despite all the work that had gone into making English radio communication so free from misunderstanding, he still found that half of what we Brits said to him in conversation was totally incomprehensible. He added that although he was a fluent English speaker there was often a substantial part of our conversation made up of idioms. The fact he knew the word idiom and its meaning was impressive enough. He was clearly on the ball.

I was interested to learn that most countries have idioms and, at face value, they all are as ridiculous as each other. He told me the Swedish idiom 'to be caught with your beard in a mailbox' has the same meaning as our 'to be caught with your pants down'.

I thought he was barking up the wrong tree and I didn't want to let him off the hook, so I said I hadn't got the foggiest idea what he was on about, but to give him the benefit of the doubt, I would not beat about the bush, but bite the bullet, throw caution to the wind, and, truth be told, at the end of the day, he had probably hit the nail on the head. I thought my reply was going to be a piece of cake but soon realised I had bitten off more than I could chew and was flogging a dead horse. I thought I could get into my second wind, but soon realised I had run out of steam, which was probably a blessing in disguise.

He thought all that was as clear as mud.

Well, he actually said 'as clear as daylight', which just goes to show he didn't really know his idiom from his elbow.

First Come, First Served

Even on a normal day, Heathrow is so busy there is a constant stream of arriving and departing aircraft, all heroically managed by its air traffic controllers. The rate at which arriving aircraft are processed is so finely tuned that the slightest hiccup can cause significant delays, and it is the norm rather than the exception to have to 'hold' in one of Heathrow's four holding patterns.

This particular day was no exception and it was looking as if it was going to be a fairly long one. Turbulent shower clouds meant that aircraft were being vectored in an ever-changing pattern in order to be fed onto final approach. This was causing air space restrictions, leading to aircraft stacking up in the holding patterns. In each hold there will be aircraft with plenty of fuel, and there will be those with not so much. We arrived with a middling amount and so were relatively content with our lot. At Heathrow, when the delays are longer than twenty minutes, the air traffic controllers will calculate an Expected Approach Time for each aircraft: a time plus or minus two minutes when they can expect to begin their approach. And they are remarkably accurate. With this information, crews can calculate whether they have enough fuel to loiter, or whether they will have to divert elsewhere. But it's more important than that. Other rules are used to determine if the landing is 'assured' (guaranteed), and then once the Expected Approach Time has been issued, fuel set aside for a diversion elsewhere can now be used as holding fuel at your destination.

So, we were all quietly getting on with the job of going around in circles (they are actually race track patterns) and at the same time, calculating, assessing and planning. Out of the blue, a pilot from 'out of town' said in a slightly self-important manner, that if he wasn't allowed to make an approach within the next five minutes he would be diverting. It was delivered in a way that sounded half demand, half threat, and could possibly have been seen as an attempt to jump the queue.

Of course, the controller, like all British people, had DNA made up of 'sequenced queueing genes' all wrapped up in a layer of 'first come, first served'. And he was having none of it. He simply asked the aircraft to state where he wanted to divert to, and he would organise it. After a few moments the replied came back that they had found twenty minutes more fuel and they would wait it out. Fair enough.

Say Cheese

Not all aircraft on the Atlantic track system fly at the same speed. It will depend on aircraft type, scheduling requirements, or having to slot into a free position on a track. And there is quite a range of speeds. You can often find yourself overtaking, or being overtaken, by an aircraft flying just above or below you, which can provide some fantastic plane spotting moments.

Up close, the contrail patterns of a large passenger aircraft are mesmerising. Streaming out of the back of the engines at very high speeds, these cloud-like tubes rotate gently. I have seen them illuminated, blood red and the colour of a sunrise, or blown into smoke rings due to anomalies in the atmosphere.

And, of course, being so close to other aircraft provides great photo opportunities. When crossing the Atlantic, pilots have use of a dedicated chat frequency. Ostensibly it's provided so they can share information on flying conditions (turbulence encounters, for example) with all aircraft in the area. The Americans mainly use it for sharing football and baseball scores, or for asking where a particular aircraft has come from and where it's going.

This sort of conversation is purely the preserve of the Americans, as to everyone else it seems slightly frivolous and pointless. I enjoyed listening to the Americans though. Their conversations typified their character: eager to talk to anyone, and with such enthusiasm it was hard to resent the intrusion. Even when somewhat jaded at three in the morning, mid Atlantic. Anyway, during one of the daylight crossings, an American pilot used the chat frequency to tell a British registered aircraft (from another company) that he had taken some great photos of the 'Brit plane' and did they want him to email them once he had landed. It was a kind gesture and I couldn't understand why the pilots of the 'Brit plane' seemed reticent about giving the guy their email addresses. After all, who wouldn't want a photograph of the plane they were flying? After some coaxing along the lines of, 'come on you guys, these are great photos', the Brit pilots finally handed over their email addresses.

A male voice said: 'mine is, captain747@....' And then a sparrow-like, female whisper: 'and mine is lettuce_leaf@....' At this point several other British crews chipped in. They thought 'lettuce leaf' was cute, but judging by their slightly sarcastic comments, they were less impressed with the blowy 'captain747'.

As a nation, it's not the done thing for Brits to be overtly showy. Having an email address proclaiming you were a captain of a 747 was bad form. But I don't think the American pilot saw it in those terms. He simply said, 'I'll send them as soon as I can to you guys. Have a great day'. And that's one of the big differences between us and the Americans.

On the subject of Brits blowing their own trumpet: A while back, I saw an advert posted on the crew notice board by a 737 pilot who was selling a car registration plate. It was something like 'B737 XXX', and someone else had written underneath it, 'also available: SAD TWAT'.

Safe and Sound

You know things aren't quite like home when you land in an African country and are met by a man whose name starts with 'commander.' He was six feet tall and nearly as wide, built of solid muscle, and trying but failing to hide a weapon under his jacket. He was there to escort the crew through the terminal and onto the bus that would take us to the compound - sorry, hotel. With us safely on the bus, he stood up and introduced himself like one of those package holiday tour reps who manage to summon up super-human quantities of enthusiasm. He was trying to convince us that all would be well. We were not to worry, apparently, because the 4x4 behind us was bristling with his colleagues. The fact that we actually needed his colleagues made us worry all the more.

The hotel had been selected because it was in the diplomatic district and came with all the mod cons of minibar, 24-hour room service and guarded entrance with a double electric gate 'airlock' system. The gates reminded me of something you might expect to see at a maximum security prison. As the outer gates closed and the inner ones opened to allow our bus into the complex, images of exercise yards and orange jumpsuits raced through my mind.

Note to self: I must try not to drop the soap in the shower. Still, once through the security procedures the hotel was comfortable enough and the staff friendly. Our stay there was fairly benign, right up to the point where I was woken up in the middle of the night to the sound of small arms gunfire. Had there been a breakout? I rolled out of bed and onto the floor, cat crawled across the room, grabbed some clothes and went downstairs to report this to reception. With almost unnatural indifference, the receptionist told me not to worry. It was probably just a skirmish between local factions and it wasn't aimed at us.

Now I don't know about you, but my definition of a local skirmish is disagreeing with your neighbour on how tall his leylandii hedge should be, not a shoot-out at the O.K. Corral. I pointed out that whether it was aimed at us or not, there was lead flying through the air and it didn't care who it was destined for.

She insisted we would be perfectly safe.

I asked how she could possibly know that.

Apparently, the hotel had bigger guns.

Mind you, it's not just foreign climes where you can feel threatened. It's all about perception (and bottles flying through the air).

We were night stopping in Glasgow. And just to make it clear, it just so happened to be Glasgow. It could very well have been any pub in any large town in the UK. Even the high street in Richmond. Probably. Maybe.

The first officer and I had decided to go for a wind-down drink. It was a lovely summer's evening, with only moderate rain and 20mph winds. We wandered into a pub in a lesser-known part of the city, and realised our mistake the moment we set foot on the carpet. 'Carpet' being a kind description for the compost of beer, deep-fried food, and cigarette butts. To add to the welcoming atmosphere, literally everyone in the pub stopped talking as one and turned to look at us.

We were not sure if their expressions suggested 'please come and join us and have a drink' or 'we are going to have your wallets, watches and rings before dumping your bodies into the Clyde'.

With exaggerated gestures, as if we had just remembered an important meeting, we banged fingers to foreheads, turned around and made a calm exit.

And then we ran.

What A Sight

During a flying career of thirty-eight years, I experienced the sheer unadulterated joy of being able to look out onto an ever-changing world from my front row, best seat in the house. Whether it was tooling along at 160mph just fifty feet above the ground in a military helicopter, or letting the world wash by at 43,000 feet, it's been amazing. And it wasn't just the special, spectacular moments, although there have been plenty of those.

Even the everyday sights were always magical: The exhilaration of flying towards a lone cloud at 300mph, sometimes 400mph, knowing full well it's not solid but nevertheless getting a tingle of excitement as the aircraft punched through it and the world went white for a while and then, in less than a blink of an eye, the panorama of the world revealed itself again.

Or feeling utterly insignificant as I manoeuvred around a large, skulking and malevolent monster of a cumulonimbus cloud, knowing that if I got too close, we would be thrown about like a grain of sand in a stormy sea. Even at some distance, a Cb would still make its presence felt. St Elmo's Fire would crackle and streak across the windshield, mini lightning bolts of discharging static electricity.

From the flightdeck, I have often been reminded of the geography lessons from my school days. I have looked down on Greenland, at icy glaciers gouging the pyramidal peaks and hanging valleys of tomorrow, ice that will one day join the many icebergs that stretched out before us.

And the giant ox bow lakes of the ancient rivers on the plains of Colorado.

And the hundreds of tiny Maldives paradises struggling to keep their heads above water.

I have seen the thin green strip of fertile land on either side of the Nile as it cuts its way through miles and miles of desert. At night, the same view is a thin ribbon of lights in the surrounding inky blackness, proclaiming the river as the rightful lifeblood of the area.

And what a special river it is. With the river flowing from south to north and the prevailing winds in the opposite direction of north to south, the early delta dwellers could use river power to travel north, and wind power to travel south, thus aiding communication and the development of the technological marvels of early Egyptian culture.

I have had bird's eye views of Everest, Fuji, the Great Wall of China, and the Rocky Mountains. I've seen Mount Ararat, described in the Bible as Noah's Ark's final resting place. I have witnessed the great Russian Steppes and the vast emptiness of Mongolia in the depths of their freezing winter. I have flown over the Sahara, Gobi and Arabian deserts. And their antithesis, the Amazon, Nile, Mississippi, Yangtze, Tigress and Euphrates.

I have flown right over the top of the Kennedy Space Centre and Cape Canaveral, and even landed on the runway there.

I've lost count of the cities I've seen from above. At night, Manhattan from 35,000 feet is unmistakeable because its geometric streets and avenues are so instantly recognisable. Each of the island-long avenues has alternating one-way systems. Madison Avenue has northbound traffic whilst its neighbour Fifth Avenue has southbound, and on it goes, flip flopping across the city. The result is a candy stripe of alternating red and white vehicle lights, interrupted only by the silhouette of the magnificent Central Park.

And the tiny fish-shaped island of Venice with the Grand Canal lazily wending its way through the centre. From 35,000 feet there is no hint of the frantic water-based activities going on down there. Or the thousands of tourists crammed into the narrow streets. Closer to home, flying into the UK from all westerly destinations, the route took us along the south coast from Land's End to the Isle of Wight. On a clear day I would find myself being reminded of happy family days-out as the scenery unrolled beneath us.

And finally, I've flown over the top of a Red Arrows flying display whilst climbing out over Bournemouth. Watching them from above rather than below is an experience I suspect not many can lay claim to.

Night Shift

I have a love-hate relationship with night flights. On the down side, it means flying through the WOCL. That's the Window of Circadian Low, defined as a 'period between 02:00 and 05:59 hours in the time zone to which a crew member is acclimatised'. As the name suggests, it is a period when the biological clock is demanding some down time from the body. At some stage during that period, therefore, if the body is being forced to be 'up and at it', it is highly likely it's going to feel a little off.

Because the nice people at the Civil Aviation Authority know and recognise this, they allow pilots to take 'controlled rest', which is basically a 'time out' or 'power nap'. The rules say that controlled rest can be taken during a time of low workload. Mid-Atlantic, when all the planning and checking has given way to monitoring, is an ideal time. Both pilots must stay at the controls, strapped into their seats as usual, but one pilot is allowed to take their headset off and rest their eyes. But only for a maximum forty-five minutes; any longer than that risks sleep inertia, with the pilot taking too long to gather his/her wits should need be. As with all power naps, they work really well. They revitalise, and re-focus a tired body and mind. Eating a light meal and keeping hydrated also helps power through that circadian low period.

At this point you may be feeling a little cheated, and perhaps also a little horrified, to learn that having paid for two pilots to look after you at all times, one of them might be asleep at the wheel. Remember though, controlled rest only occurs during periods of very low workload, for a very short time, and the resting pilot is only a finger poke away from being back in the team. And surely it is better to have both pilots as refreshed as possible for the busy period ahead?

'But what happens if the other pilot falls asleep too?' you might ask.

Well, I've never known this happen because, by allowing and formalising alternate rest periods, there is always a fully refreshed pilot at the controls. But to guard against it, we have strict rules requiring the in-control pilot to make contact with the cabin crew at specific and regular intervals, and if they fail to do so, the cabin crew have several ways to make contact with the pilots.

The Big Dipper

During my flying career, the sunsets were consistently mind blowing. You might assume they would be the same as the ones seen from the ground. But somehow, they aren't. From our lofty vantage point there is just so much more of them, the colours more intense. You are also much closer to the illuminated clouds, or you are actually inside them; the vibrant reds, oranges and yellows invading the aircraft like some alien force.

When flying west at high latitudes, where degrees of longitude tick by at a rapid rate, we would literally chase the sun, and sunsets could last for hours. Eventually the sun would win out and it would slowly slip below the horizon casting an inky black shadow of the earth on the atmosphere above, it's curvature visible against the back drop of a nautical twilight with its infinite shades of reds, oranges and blues below.

Coming full circle to the beginning of a new day, blackness would give way to the merest hint of a horizon and once again the earth's shadow would be projected onto the atmosphere. The three twilights (dawn) would do their stuff, putting on an ever-intensifying light show.

And then, sunrise.

The merest hint of light becoming brighter and brighter, the colours building, your anticipation fit to burst like a child on Christmas Day. Suddenly, the rim of the sun's disc would appear on the horizon and the majestic fireball would start its relentless climb to the heavens. Such an awe-inspiring spectacle. Literally an everyday occurrence but a miracle all the same. I never tired of sitting in my privileged viewing gallery watching it happen. Often the climbing sun would cast its bright red rays on the contrails of another aircraft and they would stream out as if on fire against the dark blue sky

When approaching London, if the timing was right, the rising sun would suddenly illuminate one edge of the Shard, lighting it up like a Star Wars light sabre - a shining beacon of the brilliance of modern-day London.

Some pilots hated the sun's assault on their tired eyes but I just loved it. I would put on my sun glasses, and drink it all in.

Nearly There

Having completed a night-time Atlantic crossing and nearing our destination, things always get busy. Gathering information, looking for all the pitfalls and problems we might encounter and planning solutions. Reviewing the weather; runway conditions; calculating landing distance requirements. If we already know our parking stand, we can calculate how much braking to apply on the runway so as to exit at the most efficient turn-off. We check the fuel state and the effects of arrival delays; we discuss arrivals procedure; rehearse the go-around procedure; go over any technical issues that might have occurred, and passenger requirements on landing, and the myriad of other things to talk through before starting our descent. It's at this time I always made sure to eat breakfast, to refuel my brain for the busy and intense finale to come.

And it's after the relative peace, quiet and calm of the night Atlantic crossing, that we collide with the full force of London Area Control Centre (LACC). A slight misnomer because LACC manages all en-route traffic over the whole of England and Wales (Scotland have their own). Suddenly, the pace picks up ten-fold. It's very busy airspace, where controllers are not only shepherding transiting traffic destined for Europe and beyond, but also cajoling the incessant stream of aircraft destined for the major UK airports.

We are now one of hundreds of aircraft being told to slow down, speed up, turn or descend, bringing some semblance of order to this arriving swarm. It's as if we are part of an out of tune orchestra, suddenly coaxed into playing a fine melody. For us, this stage of the flight is all about energy management. Most of the flight is behind us and so we have burnt most of our fuel, but we could still weigh around 215 tonnes. And at 500mph the aircraft carries vast amounts of kinetic energy. This piece of flying hardware must be kept reined in, and we must start descending and slowing down early enough to arrive at the right place and at the right speed requested by the controllers. Closing in on our destination, we are handed over to the airport controllers who fine tune the traffic sequence even further. At all UK airports we practice the Continuous Descent Approach (CDA) technique where, from roughly 8,000 feet, ATC gives each arriving aircraft the total distance to touchdown. These tracks are usually curved or 's' shaped and about twenty-five miles in length. Pilots then create and project a 3D mental model of the ideal flight path, in terms of speed, height at points along this imagined line, as well as flap and gear (undercarriage) selection points. Get these projections right (and it's a matter of professional pride that we do) we can fly the entire approach without having to level off. This keeps power levels low, saves fuel and reduces pollution and noise disturbance for those living under the flight path.

I've always found the approach and landing to be most intense and challenging part of a normal flight. Distilled down to basics, during a take-off there is the whole sky to aim at. For the landing there is no choice but to find a very specific point on a very specific line of asphalt on the earth's surface. It's bread and butter stuff but nevertheless it requires skill and concentration. And it provides an adrenaline kick that lasts until the drive home.

The final hurdle, having been awake for the better part of the twenty-four hours, is to get home safely, but not necessarily in one go. One first officer tells of being woken up by the police tapping on his car window. He was fast asleep on the motorway hard shoulder, engine still running, with no recollection of stopping the car. One captain told me he had woken up to see trees flashing past his car window. He had fallen asleep at the wheel, his car had left the road and ploughed into a wood. Amazingly, he had missed every single tree.

My solution to staying awake on the way home was to keep the adrenaline pumping by driving really fast. It always worked, but I would arrive home so hyped-up, I would start gabbling incoherently. Pen, who was used to seeing me in this state, would listen patiently to the tsunami of nonsense until, after about ten minutes, the adrenaline would start to dissipate and, like a raging rhinoceros suddenly succumbing to the sedating dart of a vet, I would collapse into an exhausted heap, fit for nothing but a darkened room.

And It's Goodbye From Me....

I've always thought one sure way of becoming a millionaire is to begin life as a billionaire and then start an airline. The airlines are constantly battling some crisis or other, and it's Darwinian as to whether they keep going or not. Survival of the fittest is the over-riding rule here.

From operating my first commercial flight to Africa, all those pages ago, I managed exactly six weeks before the economic fallout from the [first] gulf war made its mark on my career. The airline had to make savings and chose to suspend the TriStar fleet. My manager rang me at home and explained I was being stood down for an unknown period of time. Apparently, I wasn't to worry as, thanks to a deal between the company, our union and the pilots, my job was safe and I would still get paid. The pilot community looking after one another was a recurring theme over the next thirty years.

The manager ended his call by saying I would definitely, absolutely, never fly the TriStar again, and I might as well throw all my manuals away. He would look at a new fleet for me when things picked up.

You can imagine how grateful I was to be kept on, and I've never forgotten the way the pilots selflessly agreed to protect jobs. Just over six months later, the same manager contacted me to say I was to report back to work, and by the way, did I still have those TriStar manuals!

After the Gulf War and the recession in the early 1990s came the dot-com crash, followed by 9/11, SARS, bird flu, mad cow, and foot and mouth disease. The second gulf war was still being fought when, in 2008, the global financial crisis rocked the world. Swine flu followed that, and then the eruption of Iceland's volcano brought European airspace to a standstill. Bird flu returned in 2013, then came Ebola, MERS and Zika.

It's a miracle there is an aviation industry left, but it has dealt with every single crisis head on and bounced back every time.

And then the big one happened. Coronavirus, of course. It proved to be the biggest challenge ever to face the airline industry. Ever. Many airlines have ceased to exist, and the rest struggled to survive. In the first half of 2020, our company took the unprecedented step of announcing it needed to lose a quarter of its pilot workforce, first through voluntary measures and then compulsory means. Our union issued a clarion call to its pilots. Every voluntary retirement would save a compulsory one; the take-up of part time contracts would save jobs; and a deal would be negotiated with the company to place up to three hundred 'stood-down' pilots in a holding pool, on reduced salary, until things improved. This pool would be paid for by the remaining pilots, as part of a twenty percent pay cut. Once again, the pilot community rallied, and voted overwhelmingly to endorse the proposal. The pilots were, once again, looking after their own.

Having just celebrated thirty years with the airline, I thought back on all those years when my fledgling career could have gone either way, but had been saved. And I decided it was the right time to repay that debt. Time to hang up my hat. I applied for voluntary retirement.

Tragically, despite all the voluntary measures there were still some compulsory redundancies. But hopefully, right now, because of the collective actions of the pilot community, there are some young pilots sitting on the flight deck who might not otherwise be there. And perhaps they are thinking how lucky they are to be doing this job of a lifetime.

I hope they can spend the next thirty years of their lives doing and seeing some extraordinarily special things.

I know I did.

Printed in Great Britain
by Amazon